Artists: PROSPER!

Make *peace* with your *brain*
and *money* + *joy* with your *art*

CHRISTY STRAUCH

Artists: Prosper!
Make Peace With Your Brain and Money + Joy With Your Art

ISBN Paperback: 978-1-7347365-1-9
ISBN E-Book: 978-1-7347365-2-6
Library of Congress Control Number: 2021921925

Creative Peace Press
For more information on Christy and her work, please visit www.christystrauch.com

To all the creative people who want to get their work into the world with minimum trauma and maximum joy.

To Michael Hateley,
Thank you for your work in the world.
Christy Strauch
December 2021

Table of Contents

BEFORE

Stuck, Fearful, Confused, Hiding

An artist sits down to create. We don't need to know what she's going to make; we just know that the process of creating has started.

A bird flies in the window, clutching a piece of paper in its claws. (I know. Birds don't fly into our homes very often, and they never show up gripping a piece of paper. Be patient and you'll see where this is going). It's an owl.

Who are you?" the artist asks. "I never had an owl fly into my house before."

"I'm your Muse," says the owl.

"Convenient," says the artist. "I'm ready to make something. But I don't know where to start."

The owl says, "I'm glad you asked. Here are twelve ideas."

He releases the paper, and it drifts to the floor. The artist retrieves it. It's a list of potential projects.

"Thanks," the artist says.

"There are hundreds more where those came from. You'll never lack for ideas for projects. I'll always be here to supply more."

"Which one should I pick?"

"The top one. Start there and see what happens."

The artist nods, smiles to herself, and readies her tools to start.

"Don't forget. I'm always here. All you have to do is ask." The owl turns and flies out the window.

Suddenly, a small creature appears. He's wearing an elfin hat and has a huge tool belt strapped to his waist.

"Who are you?" asks the artist, eyes wide.

"I'm your inner Maker," replies the elf. "I'm the part of you that knows how to make what you're about to create. I'm your education, experience, and talent rolled into a compact, competent package."

"You're just in time," says the artist. "I was just getting started."

"Let's take a look," says the Maker. He jumps onto the back of the chair where the artist is sitting and begins giving advice about where to start.

As the artist picks up her tools to begin, the room suddenly grows colder.

"What's this?" she wonders, looking over her shoulder.

She feels slimy tentacles wrapping themselves around her wrists. As she turns to see what's happening, her wrists are already bound tightly together by the tentacles of a Jellyfish.

"Who are you?" demands the artist. "Unwrap my wrists!"

"I'm your inner Jellyfish," says the Jellyfish.

"What the hell!" the artist exclaims.

"I'm the part of you that keeps you from starting to create anything. I know you've got the idea and the knowledge and ability to make your next project, but don't you have laundry to do? What about the dishes in the sink? The car needs washing, and so does the dog, the cat, and the goldfish. Plus, there's the vacuuming. And you haven't paid the bills yet. You also need to mow the lawn, weed the garden, return that call to your mom, write that proposal, take a shower, shave your legs and your face, wash your hair, and blow dry it this time for God's sake..."

As the Jellyfish natters on and on, the artist realizes that the tentacles, now wrapped around her forearms, are beginning to sting. As the Jellyfish rattles off more and more tasks that need to be done, people to call, bills to be paid, the venom penetrates her body, spreading a sticky paralysis. She wants to stand up and go put that load of laundry into the washing machine, but she feels exhausted and lethargic. *Maybe I'll start the creative project tomorrow*, she thinks as her eyes begin to close.

Just as she's about to succumb, she sees the project list that the Muse left for her. A spark of anger flashes in her brain and she stands up.

"Get out of here," she yells, waving her arms. The Jellyfish tentacles release, and suddenly the artist is free.

"I'll be back…" the Jellyfish promises. "Don't forget about the laundry." It drifts out the open window.

The artist sits down, picks up her tools, and with renewed resolve, begins to create. The process unfolds for her, and she finishes the project.

"There," she says as she cleans her tools. "I finished." As she gazes at her work, she hears pounding. She turns to see a giant gavel has entered the room and is hammering everything it sees.

"No, no, no," it yells. "That's simply not good enough. You need to go back and fix it. You think you're so creative, but you're a fraud. Look at that thing you made. You made better work than this in sixth grade." The pounding continues.

The artist slumps in her chair. "I'm afraid to ask. Who are you?"

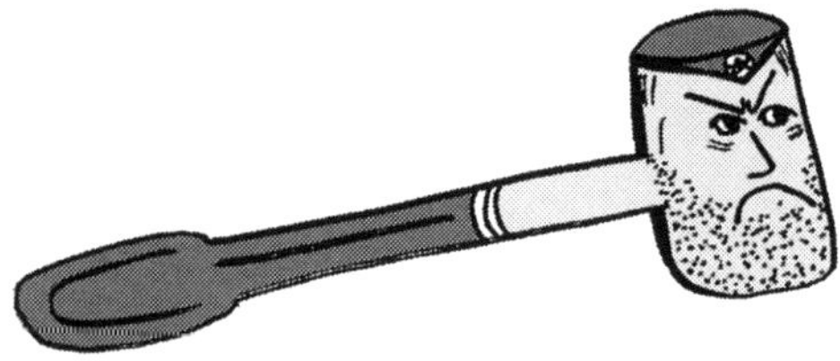

"I'm the Judge. I'm the part of you that knows you're an imposter. You might be able to keep this information from other people, but you can't hide it from me. Your work stinks. You're a poseur. You'll never be good enough."

The artist slumps further in her chair. "You're right. I am an imposter. I'll never be good enough, just like my high school art teacher said."

"I'm glad you agree," blasts the Judge. "Give up now."

As tears drip from the artist's closed eyes, she remembers the Jellyfish. *Wait a minute. That Jellyfish was wrong. Maybe this Judge is too.* She gets out of her chair and walks over to stand in front of the Judge. "Who are you, anyway?" she yells, "Go away!"

The Judge blinks in surprise. "Really? Oh, okay. I'll go." But as it floats out the open window these words drift back into the room. "Your high school art teacher was right."

"Weird," says the artist. She shakes her head to dispel the Judge's words and returns to look at what she made. "Not bad," she says. "I need to show it to some people to see what they think."

The open window slams closed. The door to her studio shuts with a bang. She hears the deadbolt lock.

Then a voice pipes up. "You're not leaving this room until you promise not to show your work to anyone." A giant skeleton key has locked the studio door and appears to be the origin of the voice.

This is like the Dickens novel, A Christmas Carol, except most of the spirits visiting me are malicious.

"Who are you?" the artist asks, weariness in her voice.

"I'm the Jailer. I keep you and your work hidden so no one can see it."

"Why would you do that?"

"Think about it. What happens when you show your work? Two things. Criticism, or silence. Remember how criticism feels? Remember how bad silence feels? You want to experience those feelings again? I don't think so."

The artist sighs, "It's not always like that. Sometimes people appreciate what I make."

"You can't risk it. It's too painful."

The artist slips to the floor in despair. *She overcame the Jellyfish's resistance and the Judge's judgment. But the Jailer is right. Rejection and silence are too painful to face.*

Suddenly, the artist hears trumpets in the distance. The window flies open again. An old woman floats into the room.

The artist can barely raise her head, but she asks, "Who are you?"

"Get off the floor, and I'll tell you," the old woman says.

The artist groans as she pulls herself into her chair. "Okay. I'm listening."

"I'm your Mentor," says the old woman.

The artist sits up and cocks her head. "My what?"

"Your Mentor, silly." The old woman pulls up a chair next to the artist and reaches to hold the artist's hands. "I'm the part of you that is connected to your creativity, connected to the flow of ideas, to other artists, to the planet. I'm the mystical part of you that helps you remember who you are, helps you remember how important your art is, and how important your contribution to the world is. I'm the part of you who knows how to ignore all reactions to your art, except your own—the only one that counts."

The artist starts to weep. "You're a part of me?"

"Absolutely," says the old woman. "You see and hear me, right?"

The artist nods.

"Good. Let's take a look at what you made."

Their heads lean together as the artist and the Mentor turn to the work.

Did you recognize yourself in this not-a-total-fairytale? Maybe you haven't called the feeling of needing to clean the house or wash the car instead of starting on your art your inner Jellyfish, but does the description sound familiar? Did you recognize the voice of your personal Judge, commenting on the futility and insignificance of everything you make? Could you relate to the fear of being seen, the reason your inner Jailer tries to make sure you stay hidden? And have you recognized your inner Muse bringing you endless ideas for new projects? Or your inner Maker who knows how to make them, and your Mentor, knowing what you're up to in the world?

If so, you're in the right place. You are an artist, and your work needs to get into the world. You deserve to make money and joy with your art.

To make this happen, you'll need two skills.

First, you'll need to know how to ***make peace with your brain***. You'll learn how to quiet, then work with the inner Jellyfish, Judge and Jailer so you can make art. All you need is an open mind, your bountiful imagination, and a skill you perfected in kindergarten; the ability to make friends.

Second, you'll need to learn how to ***make joy*** (along with some money) ***with your important, precious art.*** To do this, you must find the people who need your art, make relationships with these people, and help them buy from you, so you can prosper as an artist. These skills can be learned, and in Part Two of this book, I'll share the skills you will need.

Why do any of this? Why not just make art and see what happens? Two reasons: You matter, and your art matters. Probably more than you know.

Let's work together to clear the way for your art to do what it is meant to do in the world.

"If I am not
good to myself, how
can I expect anyone
else to be good to me."
~ Maya Angelou

Photo by Bekky Bekks on Unsplash

PART ONE

Make Peace With Your Brain

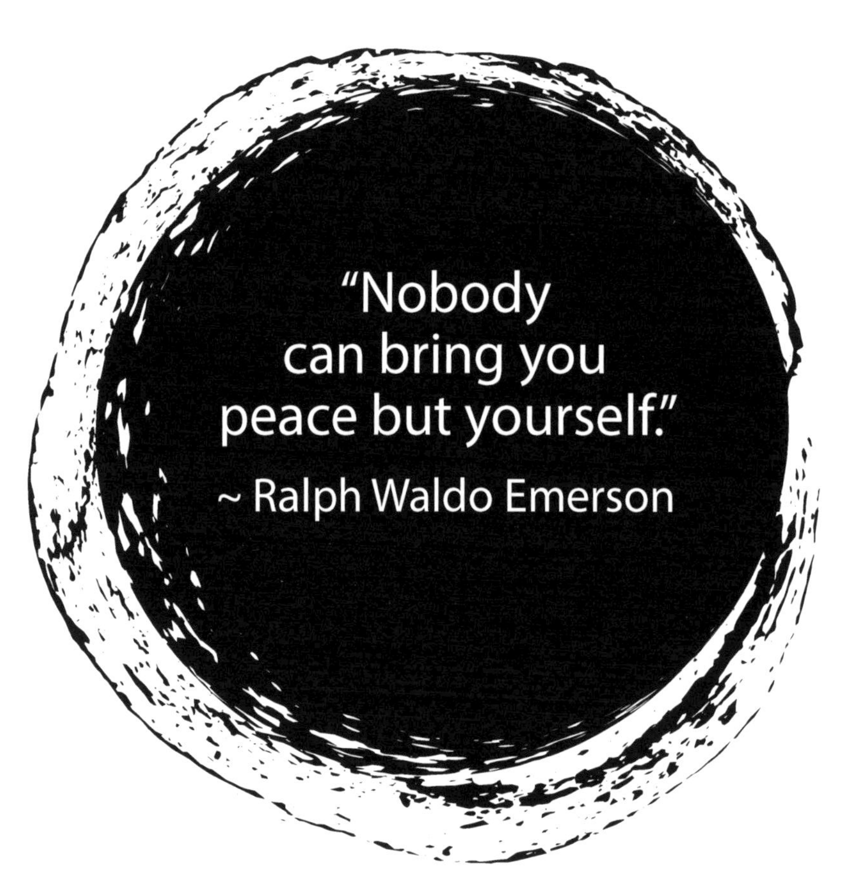
"Nobody
can bring you
peace but yourself."
~ Ralph Waldo Emerson

You're a creative genius. I know it's hard to claim that title consistently, or ever, but you are. You have something to say, emotions to evoke, people to provoke, beauty to invoke (okay, I'm getting carried away with rhyming words). My point is, what you do matters, for yourself and the people who need your work in the world. On some level, you know this, or you wouldn't be reading this book.

Being a Creative Genius Has Its Perks

You get to make/perform/write/speak/paint/sculpt amazing things. You get to bring work into the world that no one has seen before. You get to participate in the universal flow of creativity. You bring joy, excitement, amazement and change to the world. You're part of the birthing of new ideas and breakthroughs, part of changing the culture, providing beauty, clarity and light to the planet.

The Downside Is That You Have Voices in Your Head

You know those voices. The ones that say, "Of course you can do your art. But clean your desk/tidy your studio/call your brother/sort your socks first. THEN you can start." Or that say, "Good try, but not good enough. You can't quite pull off what you're trying to accomplish. No reason to waste your time working on THAT anymore." Or, "For God's sake, don't show THIS to anyone. You'll never live it down."

You're probably also painfully aware that these voices rarely rest. They keep up a running monologue of the awful thoughts that make you feel like your limbs are made of lead, that it's too hard to get out of bed, let alone compose or build or produce anything. There's no use in trying and anyway, don't you need to sew all the missing buttons on those shirts you've been hiding in your closet for the past five years?

Whatever It Takes, These Voices Are Determined to Keep You From Making Anything

If you have tried to put your art into the world, you already know what it feels like when you don't have a peaceful brain. The voices are relentless. Maybe they're soft and insidious, or loud and profane. Or maybe they change tactics depending on the circumstances. In any case, you know what it's like when those voices try to stop you from starting, keep you from finishing, or prevent you from showing your work to anyone. I'm guessing you're already well-acquainted.

Does Any of This Sound Familiar?

Do you have a stack of almost finished paintings *(It's just about the process, right? I don't actually need to finish them, do I?),* or a couple of books on your laptop you haven't touched for a year *(my best friend hated both of them so there's no point in continuing to write, is there?)*, or an idea for a cartoon you haven't been able to sit down and start working on *(my drawing skills aren't quite up to par; I need to take more classes)*, or you've written songs you haven't performed, practiced your guitar but can't get yourself to join a band, or have you written a book of poems you haven't shown to anyone? If you feel like there's a boulder sitting on your chest as you read this, you know what it's like to be paralyzed by the voices in your head keeping you from starting, finishing, and showing your art. It's awful.

If you're hoping to consistently and successfully put your art into the world, you must make peace with these voices.

"Okay," you might be saying. "But what does that even mean? Make peace with my brain? How? Have you listened to my brain? These voices are loud and scary. I think they hate me. Plus, I have no idea where to start."

I hear you. I'm here to tell you that it is possible to turn those voices from adversaries into allies. I also know you can do this.

How do I know? Because I did it.

For decades I let them keep me from writing (that's my art), then when I finally did write, I let them criticize my writing harshly and block me from showing it to anyone. I did everything to combat these voices; recited the affirmations, attended the webinars, hired the coaches, read the books, did the mindfulness practices, begged the Universe....

Some of that worked long enough for me to finish some books. But nothing permanently lowered the commotion in my head. Nothing worked until I began to understand that the voices in my brain were trying to protect me and started to appreciate how they worked overtime to keep me safe.

Even though it seems strange, implausible, or weird, what actually worked was this: ***making friends with the voices in my head.*** I did this the way you make friends with anyone. I started talking to them.

Once I started conversations with these voices, I realized that working with them didn't involve yelling, denying their existence, calling them names, drowning them in alcohol, or caving in and giving up.

Making friends with the voices in your head requires three skills you already possess. First, an open mind, which you have, or you wouldn't have read this far. Second, the fundamental skill used to make your art—imagination.

And third, everything you learned in kindergarten about how to make friends.

With these three skills, you'll be able to get to know the voices, understand what they're up to, enlist their help, and grow to appreciate and admire their dedication to keeping you safe.

"Art is a
completed pass.
You don't just throw
it out into the world–
someone has
to catch it."
~ James Turrell,
Painter

Photo by Ussama Azam on Unsplash

ONE

The Protection Racket

THESE ANNOYING VOICES ARE TRYING TO PROTECT YOU. REALLY.

What Are These Voices, and How Did They Get Into My Head?

Okay, at this point you might also be thinking, *if I admit to having voices in my head, doesn't that mean I'm crazy?*

Nope. Once you start paying attention, you'll begin noticing you have lots of them, many with strident opinions about virtually every aspect of your life. Some experts say we have hundreds, maybe thousands of "parts" or voices in our brains.

It may reassure you to know that I didn't make this up. Getting to know these voices, or doing "parts work," as it's called by some psychologists, has a rich history. The Swiss psychiatrist, Carl G. Jung, brought the idea into 20th century psychology. Specific kinds of psychological therapy, notably Gestalt and Family Systems Therapy use parts work. Other psychologists, therapists and psychiatrists, notably Drs. Hal and Sidra Stone, expanded and simplified the concepts so laypeople could use them to become more aware of what drives behavior. They have trained thousands of people to use parts work to become more conscious.

But don't worry. You don't need a degree in psychology, or your own therapist, to get acquainted with these voices in your head.

To start, I'm going to introduce you to three voices that every creative I know hears every day. I'm guessing they'll sound familiar, even if you haven't named them before. These three voices make up what I call **the Safety Squad**—the parts inside every creative that believe making art is so dangerous to the artist that they go to any lengths to prevent it from happening. I'll introduce you to each of them and explain why they do what they do.

The First Character in Our Trio of Nagging, Persistent Voices, Is the Jellyfish

Its superpower is invoking resistance. Its primary message is some variation on the theme of "You don't need to do your art right now. You need to (pick one): mow the lawn, go grocery shopping, do the dishes, pick up the kids, drop off the kids, walk the dog, clean the house, reorganize the garage, clean off your desk, clean out the hall closet, clean off the kitchen counter…"

These are all worthy tasks, and of course I don't want you to abandon your children or the dog. However, the worthiness or importance of all these tasks isn't the issue. The Jellyfish dangles them in front of you, working to convince you that they all need doing *Right Now*. This is its clever (and highly effective) strategy to keep you from picking up your brush or your camera or your ukulele or your pen or pencil, or putting on your tap shoes, and making something. It wants to keep you from starting anything.

Ironically, Jellyfish don't have a brain, a heart, or a backbone. They do, however, have stinging tentacles that release venom to paralyze their prey. *You are the prey.*

Next: The Judge

If by some force of will you do make something, the next voice chimes in. It's an old friend who probably appeared in middle school—the Judge. Once you've made something, or even started to make something, the Judge does what it does best: judges.

This criticism takes innumerable forms. It may sound like your mother or your high school art teacher, your ex, or (God forbid) your current partner, all of whom expressing some version of, "You could have done that better if only you...." Maybe you've read about the almost universal human condition called "imposter syndrome," and your Judge has jumped on that idea. "Yes, that's you! You're an imposter!" Or it compares your work to someone else's (preferably someone who just won the Nobel Prize for something), pointing out how your work isn't quite up to that standard.

Just like the Jellyfish, the Judge can sound semi-reasonable. Maybe you *should* edit the chapter one more time or touch up the corner of that painting or re-draw the last panels on your cartoon. Whether that's true or not, the Judge will use it or any other criticism it can devise, to keep you from finishing anything.

Finally: The Jailer

If by a magical combination of drive, encouragement, or sheer stubbornness, you finish something and decide to show it to someone, the third voice will pop up, the Jailer.

The Jailer's job is to convince you that showing your work to anyone besides the goldfish is dangerous and you'd better not. The Jailer may sound like this, "Did you see what happened on Instagram when your friend posted the photograph of that painting she was so proud of? Do you want that to happen to you?" Or, "No one is going to care about the composition you just finished. There's no point in playing it for anybody."

As a trio, the Safety Squad wants to keep you from starting, finishing or showing your work. They'll say almost anything to accomplish their goals.

Pretty demotivating, debilitating, and downright cruel, right? Who would ever want to get acquainted with voices this awful? Why aren't we trying to snuff them out instead of getting to know them?

An even better question, why do you have voices in your head that seem dedicated to preventing you from doing your art, the thing that brings such joy and meaning to your life?

One Word: Trauma

Many creative people have experienced trauma around their art.

I know that's a sweeping generalization. Perhaps that didn't happen to you. If you were lucky, your parents and teachers were supportive and encouraging of your art when you were young. But if they experienced criticism or silence around their own dreams, it's challenging for them to see you headed for the same painful fate. Maybe they can protect you from that pain by discouraging you now when the stakes are lower.

Maybe you experienced deeper trauma. Perhaps your caregivers or teachers weren't encouraging or supportive. Maybe they were outright cruel. Maybe they shamed you for being a dreamy, creative kid. Maybe you got punished for doing art instead of finishing your math homework, or a teacher you respected said you'd never make it as a musician/writer/dancer, or your family didn't understand or worse disparaged the value of art and criticized you for caring about it.

Then there's the dominant culture itself. Maybe if you live in France or Italy where the arts are more highly valued, you can escape artistic trauma, but not so much in North America. Tell anyone you're an artist and their first question will likely be, "Can you make any money at that?" You might have heard things like, "I don't understand modern art/music/dance/poetry," followed by a comment about how unnecessary art is, what a luxury art is, or "My kid could have done that."

You learn that you can pour your heart and soul into something, make something deeply meaningful to you, and be completely misunderstood by other people, who don't like or care or comprehend what you're doing, and will gladly tell you so. It hurts when people tell you that what you made, a creation that came from your heart and soul, doesn't matter.

If that isn't enough, we now have social media, a place where everyone's an expert. People are happy to tell you what you're doing wrong. Being attacked by haters is painful. We often pile on the pain by negatively comparing ourselves to every other artist out there.

Your Brain Learns Early That It's Not Safe to Make Art. So, It Creates a Safety Squad to Keep You From Making It

These voices' only job in life is to keep you safe. They're so obsessed with your safety that they will do the one thing that hurts you the most to guarantee it. *They'll keep you from making art.*

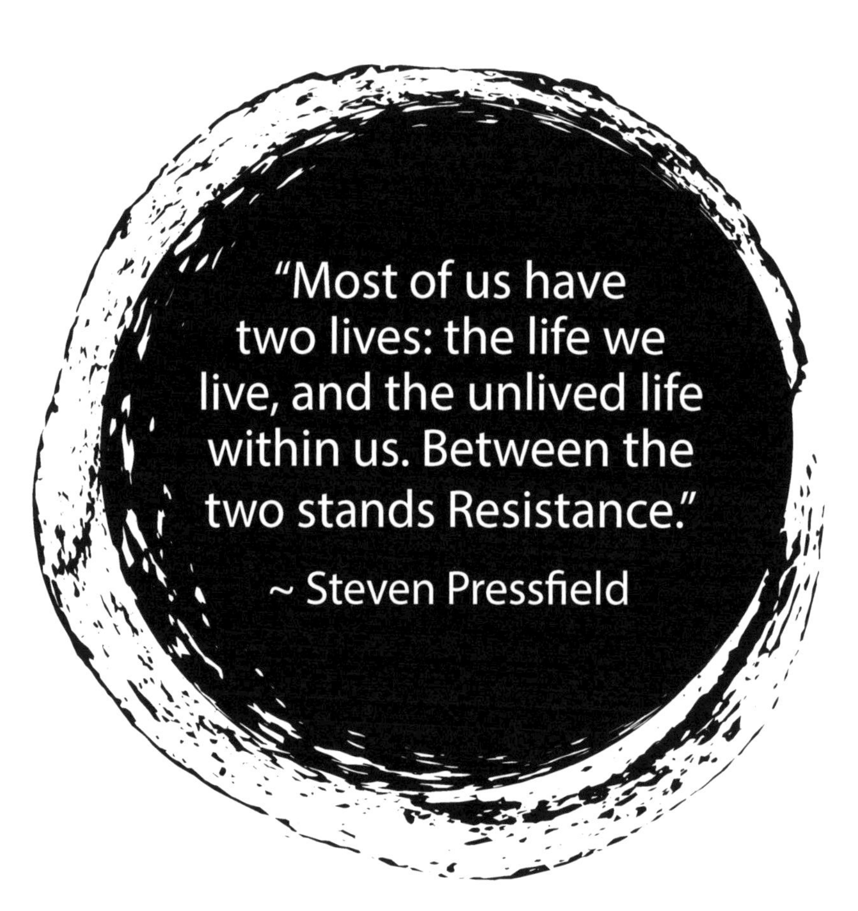
"Most of us have
two lives: the life we
live, and the unlived life
within us. Between the
two stands Resistance."
~ Steven Pressfield

Wait...Am I Saying That These Voices Are Trying to Help You?

Yes, they are. As strange as it may sound, your Safety Squad tries to keep you from getting your heart broken. Think about it. All three of these voices are obsessed with a single task. They're dedicated to preventing you from taking one of the riskiest actions in the world besides falling in love, and that is starting, finishing, and showing your art. Why? Because getting your work into the world exposes you to two perils: debilitating criticism or silence.

Your Brain Is Trying to Keep You From Experiencing Any More Trauma

This is why you can't permanently turn off the voices in your brain. Nor can you turn down the volume for very long by reciting affirmations, getting the perfect accountability partner, attending webinars, seminars or live programs that promise to teach you the five ways to beat resistance (the Jellyfish), the ten steps to silencing your inner critic (the Judge), or the six-step process to heal your fear of visibility (the Jailer). The Safety Squad's mission, to keep you from experiencing trauma, is much too important to falter in the face of wimpy affirmations or a measly ten-step process.

Affirmations and processes are fine, and they might even work for the person who's never experienced trauma around their art. But because these methods don't address underlying trauma, they won't silence the Safety Squad. The only way to win the battle between you and the Squad is to realize everyone is on the same side.

What Works Isn't War. It's Peace Talks

I hope you'll give up the war inside your head and replace it with something that actually works—***peace talks***. Don't worry. You don't need to rent a room at the U.N. and convene the nations to accomplish this. All you need is a computer, or a piece of paper and a pen, and your brain.

Peace talks go like this: you talk to these voices in your head to find out what their deepest fears are, what they're trying to protect you from, what motivates them, and what they want most for you. When you initiate these peace talks and begin to understand what the Safety Squad is trying to do, they realize that you aren't the defenseless kid you once were. They begin to relax their grip.

Your Safety Squad took on the responsibility to protect you when you were young, and they've been preventing you from making your art any way they can, not noticing you don't need the same kind of protection you did when you were six or ten or fifteen. Making friends with them is the way out of this circular trap.

But How?

If you're anything like me, right now your brain is screaming, "How exactly do I do this?"

The answer is to start having dialogues, in writing, with your inner Jellyfish, Judge, and Jailer. Talk to them, and let them talk to you, just like you would with a friend. From dialogue comes knowledge; from knowledge comes compassion, understanding, and peace.

You'll learn how to conduct these dialogues in the next chapter, then you'll have a chance to talk to your own personal Safety Squad. You'll discover what they're afraid of, what they're trying to protect you from, and most importantly, how you can begin to cooperate with each other so you can make peace with your brain and make money + joy with your art.

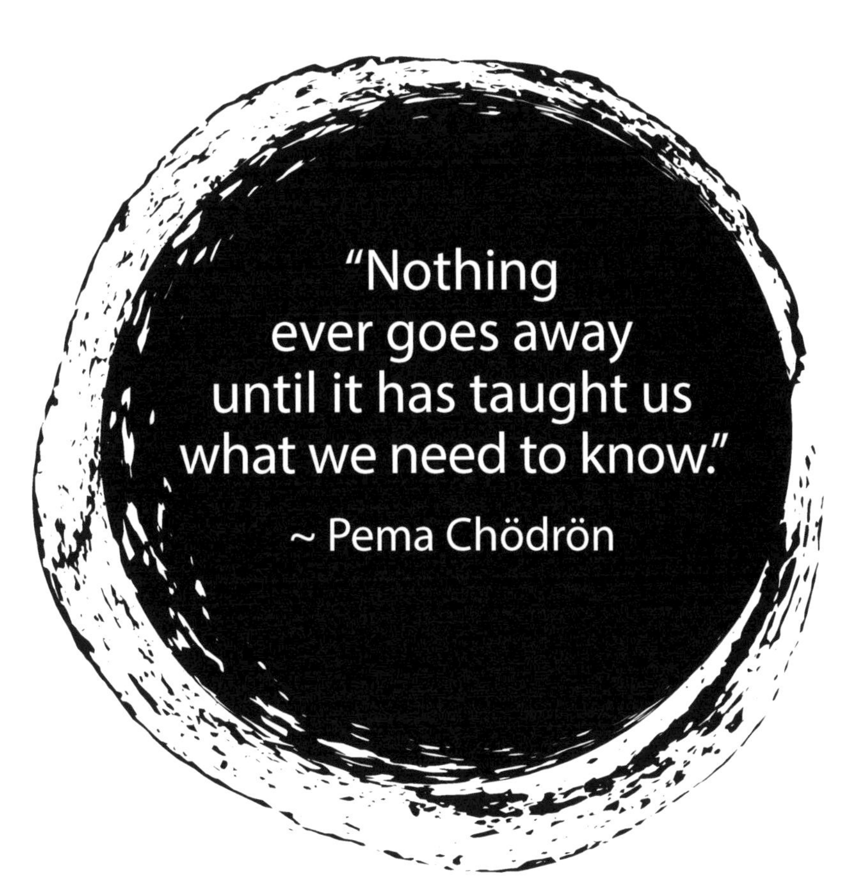
"Nothing
ever goes away
until it has taught us
what we need to know."
~ Pema Chödrön

Photo by Nelson Ndongala on Unsplash

TWO

Smokescreens

HOW THE SAFETY SQUAD USES MONEY AND TIME TO KEEP YOU SAFE.

The Safety Squad Doesn't Just Show Up When You Start to Make Art

Oh no. There are lots of devious and reasonable-sounding messages whispered in your ear during the day to prevent you from doing art. Some of the most destructive messages are those that keep you off-balance with money. I'm devoting a chapter to them.

The Safety Squad Uses Two Kinds of Money Issues as Smokescreens

The first way they throw you off balance is by reinforcing the myth of the starving artist.

The Jellyfish, in trying to keep you from making art in the first place, might say something like this: "No point in starting to make anything; you'll never sell it anyway."

The Judge has probably whispered some lies about money into your ears that might sound like this: "Your art isn't worth much." Or, "People will never pay THAT for your art."

The Jailer might chime in with, "Too risky to try and sell your art. What if no one buys?"

This disparagement of the worth of what you do can lead directly to trouble earning money. It's true; maybe you won't end up supporting yourself with your art, but devaluing messages planted in your brain turn the normal work of making money, through your art or a day job, into a slog up Mt. Everest. If that's not enough, the culture reinforces the idea that the word "starving" is inextricably tied to the work of being an artist.

Another lie you may have heard, especially from the Judge, is that you're too creative to understand business and handle money.

Let's explode that myth right now. "Handling money" requires second grade math. Think about it. You only need to know addition and subtraction. You might need some multiplication and division occasionally, but the math you mastered by the age of seven is all you need to handle money.

Understanding business takes a bit more skill and it can be challenging to figure out how to price your art, track your sales, pay taxes, etc. ***but***, you can do this too. There are whole industries dedicated to helping you, and again, you only need simple math to understand all of this.

Why Are Messages About Money So Paralyzing?

Because they have a ring of truth to them. Let's look at how your experiences with money and your art have shaped your relationship with both, and why it's so easy for the Safety Squad to use money to frighten you away from your art.

Fair Warning: These next few paragraphs dive deeply into issues with money and art. Notice what happens to you when you read them.

First, Almost All Artists Have Experienced Trauma Around Money

It's not enough to have experienced trauma around making your art. You may also be traumatized by the insanity that is the culture's ideas about the worth of art itself. Even though worldwide sales of art of all kinds are in the billions of dollars every year, not counting sales of music or concert tickets to performances (clearly, someone is buying), it's still a challenge to sell ***your*** art.

People Often View Art as a Luxury or Something Only Rich People Buy

Even though almost every home on earth contains some kind of art, we persist in thinking that art is an extravagance or indulgence, rather than the necessity it is.

Then People Who Aren't "Your People," Weigh In

Your people are the ones who appreciate what you do and are willing to pay for it. That's not everyone. It doesn't need to be everyone, but it's human to want people to value what you make. It's hard to ignore the teacher who criticizes your piano playing or the friend who pokes fun at your painting or the random idiot who says, "My kid could make that."

Then There Are the Logistics of Actually Selling Art

If you've already tried, you may have immediately run into the difficulty of pricing. Every poem, book, ballet, sculpture, painting, and song is unique. Your work might ***look*** like something that came before, but unless you're trying to make a forgery, everything you make is new. There's no standard price list to consult.

Difficult doesn't mean impossible, but difficult means difficult. Pricing is challenging.

Once you figure out your prices, the next problem is figuring out who to sell to. This opens the door to some work you'll need to do to understand who needs your art—your True People. I guarantee you there are people who need your art, but they won't congregate on your front lawn. You'll have to look for them, and you'll have to help them find you. You have to make relationships with them and help them buy your art.

You'll need to handle the logistics of selling. You might need a website or to find the right platform to sell your work—a site that handles the downloads, payment, sales tax, and shipping.

You'll also have to walk the line between making exactly what you want to make, and figuring out what your people want to buy from you.

Did your Safety Squad just get a little (or a lot) fired up and resistant from all this?

After all, you've just finished reading the list of nearly every kind of art-related money trauma there is. It would make sense if the Squad was rebelling at the idea of facing and handling any of this. (Or even finishing this book!)

But fear not! You don't have to handle any of it right now. And when the time comes to look at your relationship with money, you'll have lots of tools to make the process peaceful and easy. It will all be worth it in the end.

Problems With Money Are Just a Smokescreen

They can seem paralyzing (and I've experienced money problems paralyzing me), but they are almost always about something deeper. The something deeper is this: the Safety Squad is using money to fan your fear of being visible as an artist. The Squad knows that as long as you're spending your time consumed with money problems you have no time or energy left to create. It's a highly effective way to silence you. This is a tragedy I want to help you avoid.

Problems With Time: Same Smokescreen

Just like with money, the Safety Squad uses messages about time to keep you from creating. Here are some that may sound familiar.

The Jellyfish will certainly bring up the list of worthy but endless tasks that must be done before you can consider sitting down to do your art. The argument that you just need to do the laundry before you can start making art sounds as compelling as it does because you ***do*** need to do the laundry. Everyone on the planet always needs to do the laundry, and all the other chores that keep us clean, dry and fed. ***Just not right now***. The truth is that these tasks won't ever be completely finished. This would be true even if you dedicated 100% of your waking life to them. Might as well do art first.

"Have no fear
of perfection, you'll
never reach it."
~ Salvador Dalí

The Judge will have something to say about how much time you set aside for your art. Often, no matter how much time you reserve, it won't please the Judge. It will either be too much ("You're neglecting your other duties!") or too little ("How do you expect to finish anything working at this pace?"). The "too little time" argument can sound compelling especially if you are working a full-time day job, have a family, or both. Truthfully, it's challenging to find time to do your art, but whole books have been completed by authors writing fifteen minutes a day. Don't fall for the idea that if you don't have four hours a day to do art, then it's not worth doing.

The Jailer may say something along the lines of, "You don't need to make art until you feel inspired. You won't get much done if you aren't in the mood." Except it never works that way. You've probably noticed that starting to do your art puts you in the mood to do art.

If you're struggling to set aside regular time for your creativity, it's probably not because you don't know how to manage your time. It's more likely that the Safety Squad is at work. Once you know trouble scheduling time for your art isn't a result of being undisciplined, or having too many responsibilities, or because you're just a bad person, you can talk to the Squad and begin to make peace.

Setting Aside the Time to Actually Make Art Is Risky

That's why the Safety Squad is going to do its best to keep this from happening. It's also why time management books mostly don't work. They help you figure out when you're most creative and give you strategies about how to carve out the time. But you already know what to do. That's the easy part. The hard stuff is working with the Safety Squad.

My story might sound familiar.

I carried around this idea that serious writers set aside two hours a day, minimum, to write. But truthfully, my Judge said that two hours was a bit lame. If I were a ***real*** writer, I'd dedicate three hours every day, preferably four.

What Actually Happened?

On the days I couldn't dedicate two hours, let alone three or four, no writing got done at all. What I had to show for my idea that I needed two to four hours every day to be a serious writer, was zero hours of actual writing.

What works for me is thirty minutes of writing daily. When I commit to this, I find the time every day. My current project stays in my head where my unconscious can work on it while I'm doing other things. And there's never more than twenty or thirty hours between writing sessions, so I finish books. My Judge grumbles once in a while that thirty minutes of writing daily makes me a lightweight. Maybe, but I'm a lightweight who finishes books.

The irony of making time for art is that when you make the time, you'll meet the Safety Squad. But if you don't make the time, you'll feel miserable. There's no way to avoid some pain. The pain and criticism you hear from the Safety Squad can be handled, and you'll learn how to do that in the next chapter. The misery that comes from not doing art can't be worked with. It's a dull, unrelenting ache that colors your entire outlook on life. Really, creators don't have a choice. You must make your art.

Here's the Good News

Dedicating consistent time to your art will make you more productive, which reinforces the whole beneficial cycle. Most important, making time for your art, tells your creative soul that it matters. Because it does.

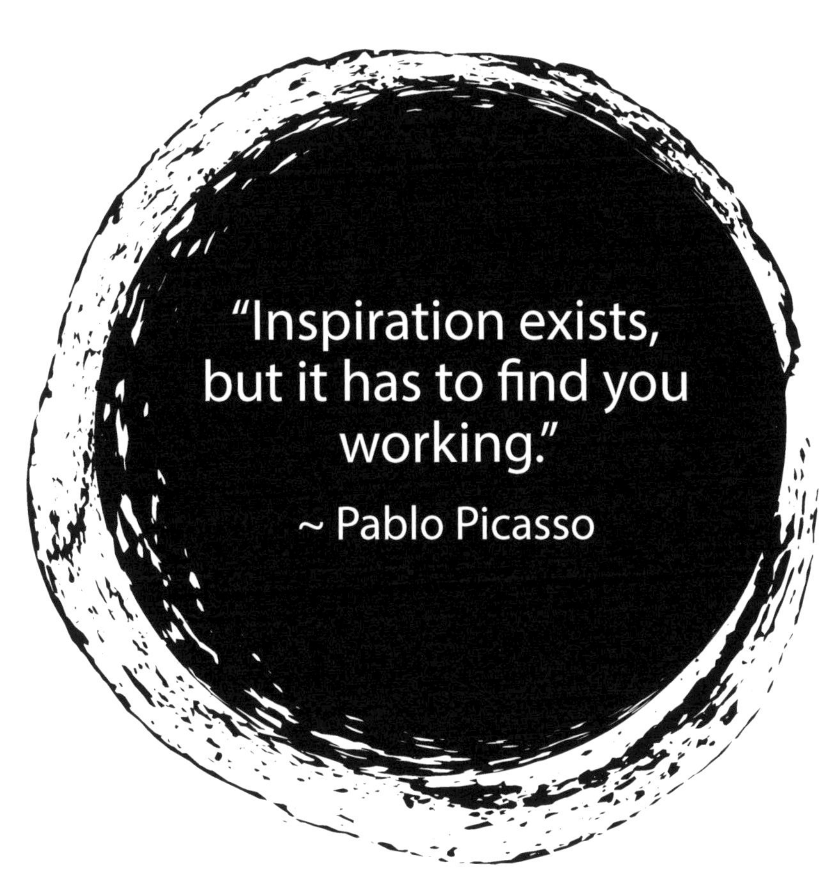
"Inspiration exists,
but it has to find you
working."
~ Pablo Picasso

Photo by Priscilla DuPreez on Unsplash

THREE

Peace Talks

HOW TO END THE CONSTANT WAR IN YOUR BRAIN.

Now It's Your Turn to Begin Your Own Peace Talks

Imagine this: You start to think about making art and, instead of the Jellyfish jumping in with a mile-long to do list, your brain is quiet, and you hear cheering in the background. Or, you make a piece of art, and the Judge sits quietly by and observes. You make your art in peace. And, when it comes time to show or sell your art, the Jailer puts away the key, and you feel free. All of this is possible when you make friends with the Safety Squad.

It's not hard. You simply imagine your own personal Safety Squad members and have a written conversation with each of them.

This may still seem weird, but if you've ever said, "One part of me wants to go to the gym, and another part wants to sit on the couch and watch Netflix," you intuitively know that you have different parts inside yourself, with different ideas about what the right thing is to do.

They're often visible when you're in conflict with yourself about something like the gym vs. the couch; early bed early vs. video games 'til 2 am; call your mother or wait another day....

You don't need special channeling abilities or to be a guru, a yogi or psychic to talk to your Safety Squad. You're just going to sit down with your questions and listen intentionally, instead of viewing them as annoying background noise, or hopelessly trying to drown them out.

When you have these Squad conversations, what works in real life with real people works when talking to your Safety Squad. Stay curious, don't argue, don't judge. It might be hard to suspend judgment of the Safety Squad; after all, they've been shouting at you for years.

Here's the peculiar thing. Under all the bellowing, you and the Safety Squad actually have the same goals—to feel accepted, approved of, and safe. Once you establish a connection with your personal Safety Squad and they begin to feel heard, you'll understand how they came to be, why the only way they know to keep you safe is to block you from doing art, and how you can all cooperate to get your art into the world safely.

A Massive Perspective Shift

Yes, I'm asking you to consider changing your entire outlook on these voices; voices you may have spent enormous amounts of time, effort, and money to silence.

It might help to understand where our Safety Squads originated.

They start to develop when two things happen together. First, we experience deeply painful criticism or punishment from people who matter deeply to us, and second, there's nowhere to turn for support, except inward. We know we don't want to feel these excruciating feelings again, so we create Safety Squads inside ourselves. Their job is to help us identify the potential for future trauma, then do everything they can to make sure we avoid doing anything that might cause criticism, punishment, and the resulting bad feelings to happen again.

As best you can, set aside any previous experience with these voices and just listen to them with kindness and compassion, without judgment, the way you'd gladly listen to a friend who needed your support. You'll be connecting to parts of yourself that have been on the job for decades, toiling alone. Instead of showing up with anger, you'll be better served if you show up with an open mind, curiosity, and a well-deserved cup of (virtual) tea.

Here's the best part. You don't have to take my word for any of this. You can try it yourself and see what happens.

Start Your Safety Squad Dialogue Now

To help you experience what a conversation with a member of your own Safety Squad might look like, I've included an example of the preliminary peace talks between my Judge and me. After this example, you'll find questions you can ask your own personal Jellyfish, Judge and Jailer.

I started with my Judge because it is by far the loudest member of my own Safety Squad and the one I have the most conflict with. You can start your own conversation in the order I've presented the Safety Squad, or you can start with the member that's the most strident, or pick the one that seems most open to conversation. It doesn't matter where you start. Just choose one and open up the dialogue.

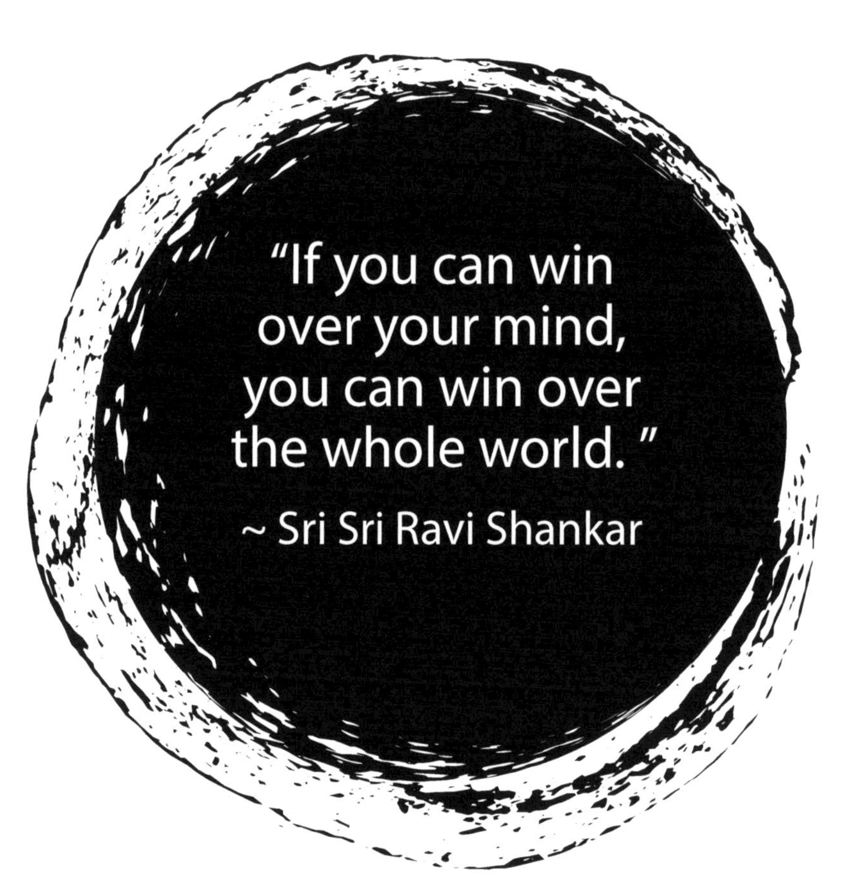
"If you can win
over your mind,
you can win over
the whole world."
~ Sri Sri Ravi Shankar

Christy: May I talk to my Judge?

Judge: Yes. As long as you're nice to me.

C: I will be. I promise. Tell me about yourself.

J: I'm the part that criticizes your writing.

C: Why do you do that?

J: I'm scared for you. Once you put out a book on Amazon, everyone in the world can see it. It's super scary. You don't handle criticism very well. You couldn't even read that one negative review about your business plan book on Amazon without feeling bad for weeks. Years, really. That review is five years old now and you still feel bad about it, don't you? [Note: this is a true story. In fact, I still cringe when I think about that review.]

C: Sort of.

J: So, I don't want that to happen to you again. That's why I'm so harsh.

C: It hurts my feelings.

J: I'm sorry about that. It just feels so scary for me to let you put your books into the world. I hate how upset you get about criticism. I want to keep you from feeling bad that way.

C: I need to write, though. How can we work out something so I can write and finish my books?

J: Well. You can be in less of a rush to finish. Let stuff sit, then go back to it and edit it again. You're always in such a hurry.

C: I'm afraid if I don't hurry, I won't finish.

J: You'll finish. You always do.

C: What's your deepest wish for me?

J: To put out the best work you can.

C: Really? I'm glad to hear that. How can I honor you?

J: Listen to me when I start talking. I know I'm harsh, but I'm trying to get your attention. Something needs to be fixed. I'm trying to tell you what it is.

C: So, listen to you, and take my time?

J: Yes. That would help me calm down immensely.

C: Okay. I can do that. Thanks for the information. I'd really like to have a peaceful relationship between us.

J: Just listen to me when I start talking and heed what I'm saying about what you need to revise. Then I won't have to yell so loud.

C: Good point. Okay. I will. Thanks.

J: You're welcome.

What did I learn here? That my Judge voice is afraid for me, for real reasons. There is a negative review on Amazon about one of my books, and I did obsess about it. The Judge wants me to make sure I do a good job on everything I write. And it's willing to calm down and not be so loud if I just agree to listen to its concerns when I begin hearing them in my head.

This Is How My Preliminary Peace Talks Went

But what's more important is how yours go. Let's find out now.

Open a fresh document on your computer or grab a piece of paper and a pen. I've listed questions for the Jellyfish, Judge and Jailer in that order, but you don't have to follow the order. Decide which part you'd like to talk to first, refer to that list of questions, and write down the first question. Then listen and transcribe the answers you hear.

If you start this exercise and nothing's coming through, try sitting in one chair, writing down the question or typing it into your laptop, then change chairs to type or write the answer to the question. Sometimes it helps to physically embody the part in a different location than where "you" are sitting. And, if you continue to draw a blank, give yourself permission to "make it up."

Don't worry about getting this right. This is a muscle that you're building. At first, I couldn't tell who was talking or if I was just making it all up. You'll gradually be able to identify the different parts by what they're saying and how you feel as you transcribe what you're hearing.

A note of caution. If a part tells you something that you know is crazy or ill-advised, disregard it. If your Judge says you will only be safe if you stop doing art altogether, that's clearly not an option and you must say so. Remember that you're always the boss.

If you'd like to start with your Jellyfish, read on. If not, skip to the part you want to start with, and begin there.

Your Inner Jellyfish

If that image doesn't resonate with you, think about this voice as the voice of resistance; the part of you that wants to keep you from starting anything. It's the voice that suggests the myriad of other possible, deeply worthy tasks you could be doing besides making your art.

Start the conversation by saying, "I would like to have a conversation with my Jellyfish." Or, "Is this a good time to talk?" If you receive a "Yes," carry on. If the part doesn't answer, or says no, move on to a different member of the Safety Squad and start there. If your Jellyfish answers a question that prompts you to ask another question not on this list, follow the thread of your actual conversation.

Here Are the Questions

How are you feeling about talking to me?

What happened to cause you to appear in my life?

What role do you play in my life right now?

When you try to keep me from starting my work, what's your motivation?

What advice do you have for me?

How can we cooperate with each other?

Anything else you'd like me to know?

Congratulations! You've begun your personal Peace Talks with the first member of your Safety Squad.

Next, let's talk to your Judge. If that image doesn't resonate, think about this voice as your inner critic. This is the voice that is never satisfied, no matter how hard or long you work on your art.

It might be even more difficult to listen without judgment to your inner Judge. After all, it has been judging you for many years; only seems fair that you might return the favor. But to understand this voice and what its deepest purpose is, as well as how it's trying to help you, it's crucial to suspend judgment. Take breaks if you need to.

I've listed some introductory questions to get the conversation started, but again, follow the thread the way you would with a friend you're getting to know. Ask permission the way you did with the Jellyfish.

Here Are the Questions

When did you first come into my life?

What do you care about the most/What are your strongest beliefs and values?

What do you worry about the most for me?

When you criticize my work, what is your motivation?

What do you want most for me?

What would my life be like without you?

What do I not "get" that you wish I understood?

How could we work together?

What advice do you have for me?

Anything else you want me to know?

Excellent work.

Personally, making peace with my inner Judge has been the most difficult. My Judge has opinions about everything, far beyond just my work. Once you start noticing your own Judge you may notice yours never rests, either. You might experience negotiating a cease-fire with this voice will bring peace to lots of other areas of your life.

This last conversation will be with your inner Jailer. Think about this voice as the one who doesn't want you to be seen, who knows that if you show your art to anyone, either criticism or crickets are the only possible outcomes. I've suggested some questions, but follow the actual conversation the way you would with a friend. Don't forget to ask permission.

Here Are the Questions

When did you first show up in my life, and what was happening then?

When do you show up in my life now?

What is your higher purpose in my life?

What do you worry about the most?

What is your superpower?

If you had your way, what would my life look like?

How can we cooperate with each other?

What else would you like me to know or understand?

Congratulations. You've Started Peace Talks With Your Safety Squad.

Making peace is the way to show them it's safe for them to loosen their grip.

Now that you know how to talk to the Safety Squad, you can repeat the process every time you get scared. You'll know one or more of them is active because they'll be trying to keep you from making art. When this happens (and it will, these are life-long companions), take ten minutes to sit down with your laptop or a piece of paper and a pen, and have a written conversation. Once they know you're willing to listen they'll begin sharing their deeper fears, and you can resolve them together instead of staying locked in conflict.

This Takes Some Practice

But I guarantee that once you begin to understand these voices have your safety at heart, the adversarial relationship will begin to dissolve. You'll start to create peace in your brain, leaving you free to make money and joy with your art.

Photo from Bigstock.com | ©1STunningArt

FOUR

Creative Superheroes

THE GOOD GUYS (AND GIRLS).

Luckily, It's Not All War and Conflict in Your Brain

The good news is not all the voices in your brain are negative. You've probably noticed you have supportive, inspirational, confident voices in your head, too. They're often drowned out by the Safety Squad, but they never disappear completely.

There's the voice that whispers, "Hey, I've got this new idea." I call this your Muse. It's the voice that comes up with new things to make, to experiment with, to mashup, to collaborate on, to create.

Then there's the Maker. This voice knows how to compose the music, paint the painting, choreograph the dance. It paid attention in art class or orchestra, or found someone to learn from, to apprentice with, to practice with. It's the part of you that knows your craft.

Finally, there's your Mentor. This voice is quiet, gentle, often hard to hear. It's the voice that knows you and your art are worthy, that you matter, and what you make matters. It's the still, small voice that connects you to the creative flow of life, and knows you're an integral, inseparable part of that flow.

These Three Voices: The Muse, The Maker, and the Mentor, Make Up the Creative Council

As important as it is to make working relationships with the Safety Squad, it's equally important to open dialogue with the Creative Council. Strengthening your relationship with each Creative Council member is another way to calm the Safety Squad, while reinforcing who you are as an artist.

Imagine Life With Your Creative Council as Active Allies

Visualize yourself sitting down with your Muse when you want to dream up a list of new projects, or figure out together which project you need to work on next, especially if you can't decide what to do first. Imagine walking away from the conversation with a list of new ideas, along with guidance about where to start.

Imagine brainstorming ways to approach a project with your Maker, who knows what you do best. Envision knowing which of your skills is needed to make your next piece look or sound the way you see or hear it in your head. Think about having an inner advisor that knows what you do well and where you might need more training or help. Think about that advisor presenting this information to you kindly and supportively.

Then see yourself sitting down with your Mentor—the part of you that knows the deepest truths about you and your art; knows the purpose of what you're doing, why it's important, and why it's needed in the world. Think about what it would be like to talk with your Mentor when you lose sight of why your work is important, when you lose confidence in yourself, and be reminded again and again why what you create matters.

What would your artistic life be like with these allies? Find out for yourself.

I've suggested some questions you can ask the Creative Council below.

For some reason, maybe because we seek to avoid pain more than we seek to experience pleasure, there's a tendency to focus on the critical voices of the Safety Squad more than spending time with the Creative Council. Maybe it's because the Safety Squad is so vociferous. I've found that spending time intentionally with the Creative Council pays huge dividends in how I feel about the worth of my work, the sense of purpose and guidance I feel about my writing projects, and the certainty that I'm on the right path. I encourage you to talk to the Safety Squad when they show up, but relish a scheduled, daily conversation with a member or two of the Creative Council. This relationship will keep you connected to your work and its worth.

If All The Answers Are Inside Me, Why Don't I Know Them Already?

You might be wondering, *If I'm carrying this information inside myself about my projects, my skills and my purpose why don't I already know it?*

It's because the Safety Squad blocked you from knowing what you know or acting on it. But you've started working with them and they've begun to relax their grip.

"I have a flood
of ideas in my mind.
I just follow my vision."
~ Yayoi Kusama

I've suggested questions but feel free to follow your intuition. Also, I'm assuming your Creative Council will be happy to talk, but if you sense reticence or shyness, remember to ask what they need to feel safe. As always, let the conversation flow naturally. You'll be surprised by the results. Get your laptop or your paper and pen, and let's get started.

Some Questions for the Muse

How do you feel about the projects I'm working on?

Are they the right ones, in the right order?

What would you change?

What do you want me to work on next?

Are these projects connected? If so, how?

How can I best support you?

Anything else you want me to know?

Some Questions for the Maker

In what areas am I most skillful?

What ideas do you have about how I could get even better with my art?

Do you have ideas or input about my current projects?

Do you have ideas for future projects?

Anything else you'd like me to know?

The Judge might show up here to tell you that you need more training in everything before you can make anything that matters. The Jailer might also appear to say that you need ten more years of education before you can show your work to anyone. If you can't tell who's talking, or the voice sounds harsh or judgmental, come back later and try again, or ask the Safety Squad to please be quiet while you're talking to the Maker. You can tell them you'll talk to them shortly.

Some Questions for Your Mentor

What is the purpose of my art?

Why do I matter as an artist?

Why does my art matter?

How can I remember this when I forget?

How can we strengthen our relationship?

Anything else you'd like me to know?

Congratulations! You've Begun to Make Relationships With Your Creative Council

Turn to them when you feel stuck, or when the Safety Squad loses its collective mind and tries to paralyze, judge, or imprison you. Consider having regular conversations with members of your Creative Council even when you aren't stuck as part of your process to stay connected to your creativity. The Creative Council can help you remember who you are, what you do well, why it matters, and how brilliant, creative, and necessary your art is.

Photo by Hello I'm Nik on Unsplash

PART TWO

Make Joy + Money With Your Art

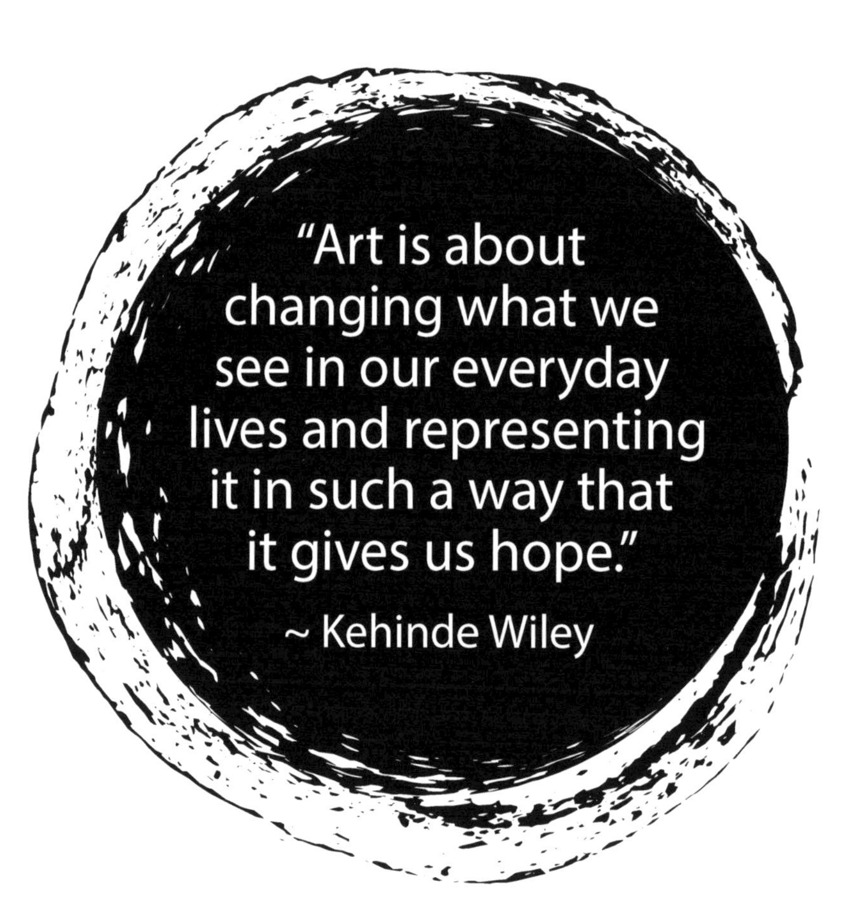
"Art is about
changing what we
see in our everyday
lives and representing
it in such a way that
it gives us hope."
~ Kehinde Wiley

Now that you've begun to make peace with your brain you've got lots of options. One is to make joy with your art. Not just for yourself, but if you want, for other people too. Another is to make money.

In this section we'll cover how to do both.

First: We'll Talk About Purpose

Your art has a purpose, a job to do in the world. Knowing what it is makes setting yourself up to earn money with your art much easier, more spontaneous, and natural. The purpose of your art and the way you talk about it will start attracting the people who want what you make. In the next chapter you'll talk to your Mentor to find out what you and your art are up to in the world.

Then: A Working Relationship With Time

The Safety Squad keeps you from doing art by convincing you there isn't enough time for your art, or you don't dedicate enough time, you spend too much time, or you're a slacker and can't manage time. All red herrings, of course. In this section you'll decide how much time you need to make your art, then set it aside with minimum drama or fuss.

Next Up: Financial Serenity

It's possible to make art in peace, secure in the knowledge that your bills are paid. Paid bills may not be sexy, but they're crucial for your creative well-being. I'll explain how.

Finally: Get Your Art Into the World

Even though you may not know who your right people are yet, there are people who need and want what you make. You'll learn how to find them, make relationships with them, and help them buy. You'll learn how to create a community around your art.

Wait. Do I Have to Sell My Art?

Nope. You can decide to make your art just for yourself. Many artists do. They create with 100% freedom, never worrying about making money.

But if you want to get your art into the world, the best way to do that is to find your people, make relationships with them, and help them buy what you create.

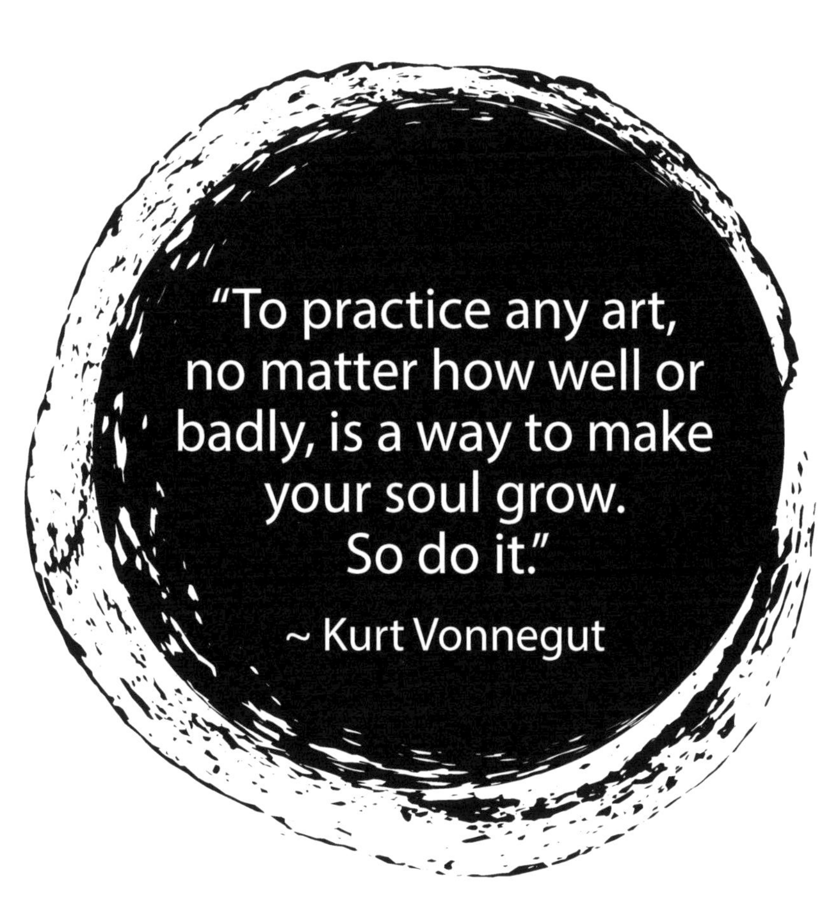
"To practice any art,
no matter how well or
badly, is a way to make
your soul grow.
So do it."
~ Kurt Vonnegut

Photo by Utopia By Cho on Unsplash

FIVE

Your Art Matters

AND YOU ALREADY KNOW WHY.
(REALLY. YOU DO.)

Let's Discover the Purpose of Your Art

Don't be surprised if you suddenly feel the Safety Squad spring into action just from thinking your art has a purpose. After all, art is just art, right? Its only purpose is to entertain. Or maybe match the sofa. Art can't help you make more money, lose weight, or find your soulmate...the only things the experts tell us truly matter in life, right?

To help calm the Safety Squad let me explain why art matters, why ***your*** art matters, why being able to articulate your purpose is useful and important, and how simple it is to find.

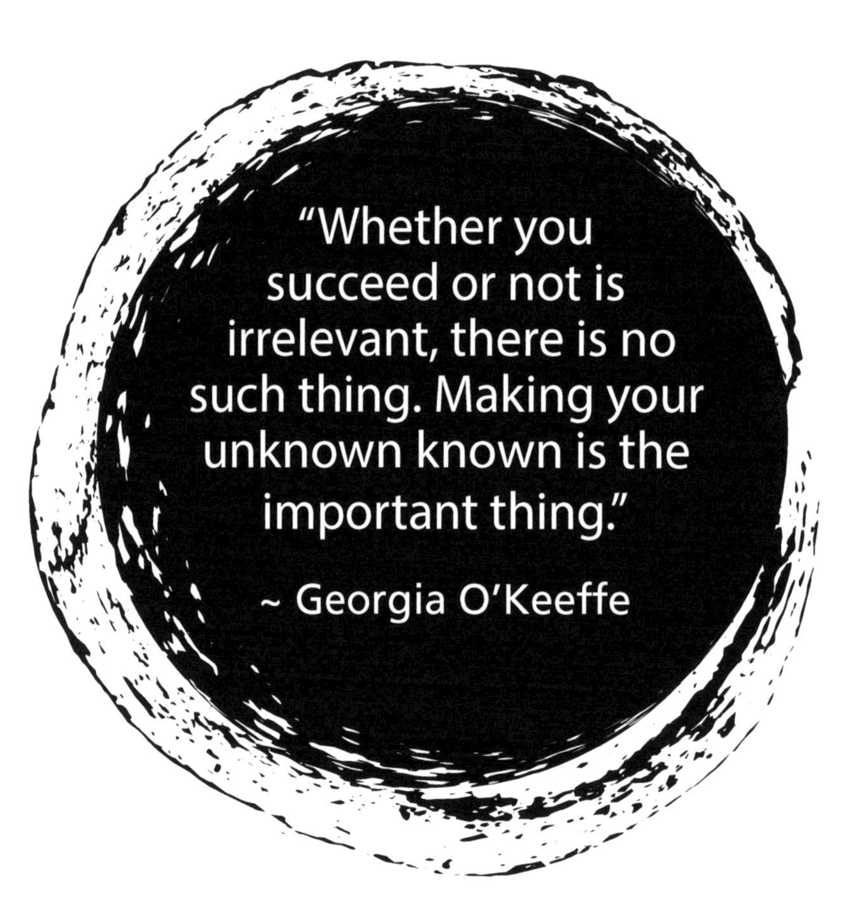
"Whether you succeed or not is irrelevant, there is no such thing. Making your unknown known is the important thing."
~ Georgia O'Keeffe

Why Art Matters

Everyone has art in their lives, their homes and ears, adorning their walls, even their bodies. But sadly, too much art out there is homogenized and commoditized. That's why ***your*** art can touch people in a deeper way than a print from a furniture store, the number one stream on Spotify, or the latest book on the New York *Times* bestseller list ever could.

Individual artists and their vision define and change culture. Artists are the canaries in the coal mine. They see the changes that need to happen long before everyone else, and start singing, painting, dancing, or playing them so the culture can begin to see what the artist sees. This is how cultures start to shift.

Why is it important to recognize that art matters? Because understanding this at a deep level will help you sell your art. You play a role in helping people see what they need to see. Knowing the importance of your role is crucial to getting your own art into the world.

What's the Purpose of YOUR Art?

Before answering this question, here are the four reasons why knowing your purpose is helpful.

First, knowing your purpose can keep you going when you are stuck, afraid, or attacked by members of the Safety Squad, or other people. For instance, knowing the purpose of your photography is to connect people to the beauty of the desert and to motivate them to take steps to preserve it, makes it easier to shrug off someone's remark about how they don't like the colors in one of your photographs. Even though it may sting for a minute, this kind of criticism becomes meaningless in the face of knowing your purpose.

Next, your purpose can guide you to work with your Muse to determine what to create. If you know your purpose is to help people be present for the beauty that surrounds them every day, this might point you to your next project, a new way to present your work, or to the next place you want to photograph.

Understanding the greater purpose of your work can also help you focus your attention outside yourself. Most artists say at least part of the purpose of their art is self-expression. Their art is a way to work through difficult issues, it's part of caring for themselves, and it's deeply personal.

There is nothing wrong with this. In fact, I believe it's an essential part of how you help the people who need what you do. You work stuff out for yourself first through the paintbrush, the song, dance, or the pen. Then your work helps others do the same.

Beware, you can get lost in doing the work just for yourself. If you're going to sell your art, remember your art isn't just for you. Other people need you to keep going. They need what you're discovering, processing and making.

Finally, the purpose of your art is information you'll use when you start talking to the people who need and want your work. I'll talk about this in a later chapter, but, for now, I want you to start thinking about your purpose as a bridge to your people. Art is a necessary, even crucial part of life for almost everyone. Helping ***your people*** understand it's ***your art*** they need requires you to be able to talk about your art in a way that is deeply meaningful, so they can connect and relate.

"But how," you might be wondering? "How the #%!# do I figure out the purpose of my art? I can't even articulate it to myself, and I'm the one making it!" Luckily, there are two simple ways to figure out your purpose. One is to use a technique called "repeating questions." The other is to have a written dialogue with a very helpful member of your

Creative Council, your Mentor. Let's start with repeating questions, then move to the written dialogue.

Repeating questions works like this. You ask yourself, "What is my art for?" then deepen your understanding by asking a single repeated question: *So that what?*

Here's how the repeating question process unfolded for a fine art photographer dedicated to the desert. 'P' is the photographer. 'A' is her art, answering the questions. Notice as she continues asking questions, she gets deeper and more detailed information.

P: What is my photography for?

A: To illustrate the rule of thirds in the composition of the photograph, and make sure it's composed perfectly so people can see the beauty of the desert.

P: So that what?

A: People can see the diversity of the desert.

P: So that what?

A: When they buy a photo, they can take a piece of the diversity and beauty home with them, especially if they don't live in the desert.

P: So that what?

A: They can maintain their connection to the landscape even when they aren't there.

P: So that what?

A: They understand they're connected to this part of the earth, that it's important, worth preserving, beautiful, colorful, varied, vital, alive.

This resonated deeply with her.

Here are the answers from a painter.

P: Why do I paint?

A: So I can make images that resonate with my heritage as a Native American.

P: So that what?

A: People who don't know about Native America, especially where I live, can start to see, and experience its importance and beauty.

P: So that what?

A: They understand we're here. That we're important, a vital part of the land, the history.

P: So that what?

A: People see our value and sacredness.

This landed in her gut.

Now You Try

Take out a piece of paper and a pen, or open a document on your computer. Ask—what is the purpose of my art? Write down your answer. It doesn't matter whether you think you landed on the right answer or not, as you can see from the repeating question examples. These two artists ended up in very different places from where they began. Ask the question, answer, and repeat the inquiry, *So that what?* Repeat the process until you land on some new information, or you feel like you're repeating yourself. You've made a start.

Next, have a conversation with your Mentor. Get out your pen and paper or open another document on your computer, and start with the questions I've suggested. The process isn't difficult or complicated. Your Mentor knows the purpose of your art and is willing to offer guidance. This gets easier with practice.

Questions for Your Mentor

What is my art for?

How can I best express this purpose?

Why is it important for me to do my art?

What impact do you want my art to have on the world?

What impact do you want my art to have on my people, the people who want and need what I do?

Anything else you want me to know?

I like to use both methods to see if I get different and/or more detailed information about why my art is important. Talking to my Mentor lets me use my imagination to discover the purpose of my art; asking the repeating question engages my logical brain to dig deeper into the purpose. I often get the best of both worlds when I use both techniques.

This Isn't an Exact Process

It helps to repeat it. Every time I do each exercise, I get more information. As you continue to practice both techniques, your answers may evolve. Mine have, although I always end up with some version of 'Helping creative people heal their money issues and get their transformational work into the world.' Lately, though, the evolution of the purpose of my art, writing, has started to include requests for elegance and beauty in my work with creativity and money.

With your purpose, or at least a working definition of it, let's move to the next step in getting your work into the world—financial peace.

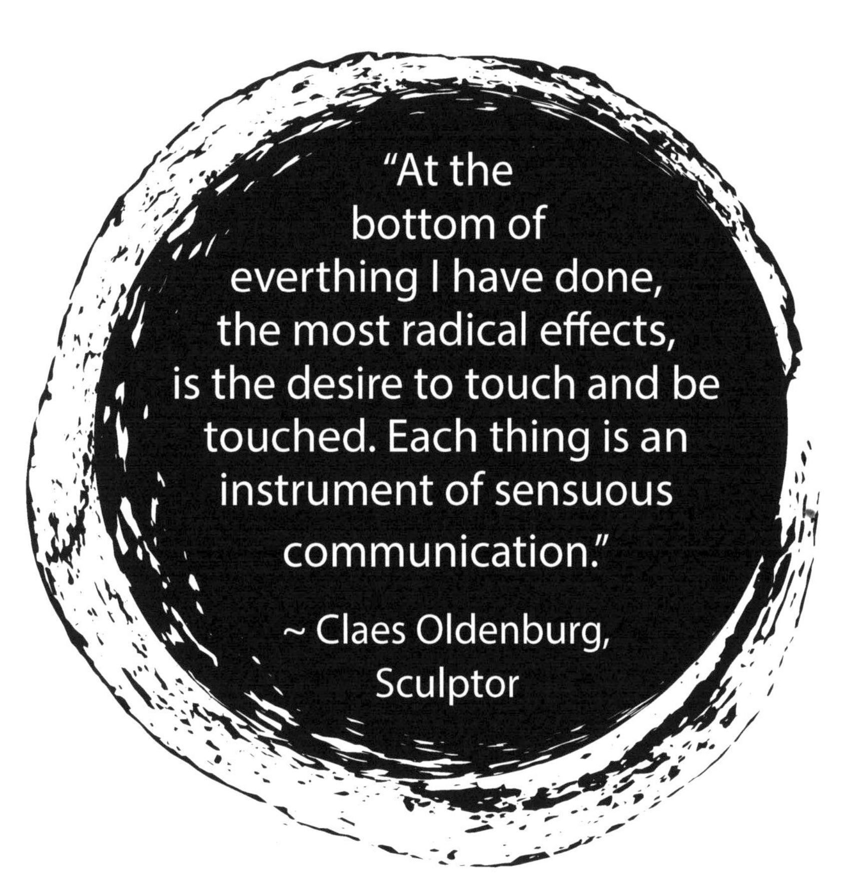
"At the
bottom of
everthing I have done,
the most radical effects,
is the desire to touch and be
touched. Each thing is an
instrument of sensuous
communication."
~ Claes Oldenburg,
Sculptor

Photo by Lori A. Johnson, Writer and Photographer

SIX

Get a Job (or Make a Job)

IN CASE YOU DON'T HAVE A RICH AUNT, WHO LEFT THE MONEY TO YOU INSTEAD OF TO HER CHIHUAHUA.

Let's Create Financial Harmony in Your Life

Contrary to the popular image of the typical artist that includes wearing holey shoes and tattered clothing, starving in an unheated garret (what is a garret, anyway?), creativity thrives in heated, comfortable homes where the utilities are always paid, the refrigerator is full, and there's gas in the insured automobile or transit cards in every jacket pocket.

If you've ever experienced financial deprivation, you already know this. If you haven't, take my word for it. Poverty is a soul-sucking experience. There is no more effective block to your creativity than the prospect of the electricity getting cut off, skipping your visits to the dentist because you can't afford them, or worrying about making next month's rent. Financial instability hijacks your brain, leaving nothing behind for your creative practice but a few stray, tired brain cells. It's impossible to do your best work under these conditions.

This means that unless you have a cooperative partner who supports you doing art full-time, a trust fund, or the rich aunt (who doesn't have a Chihuahua), you're probably going to have to get or make a day job.

Did the Safety Squad Just Report for Duty?

Is the Jellyfish telling you not to look at this chapter because a decent day job is simply too difficult to find and there's no use trying? Is the Judge yelling that you can't find a day job because you don't have the right aura? Or is the Jailer whispering that disclosing you have a day job to people will devalue you and your art so let's not discuss this right now…?

A day job will make your creative life, indeed your whole life, easier. It's also not difficult to get or make one. If any member of the Safety Squad squawks about this … oh, who am I kidding, we know they will. Let's just talk to them about this whole day job business right now.

Here's a transcript of me talking to my Safety Squad to discover any concerns they might have about me having a day job. You'll have a chance to do the same thing with your Safety Squad.

Me (to the Jellyfish): Can I ask you—are you concerned about me making or getting a day job? If so, why?

Jellyfish: I'm worried you'll get some awful job that will make you work too hard. Then you'll be exhausted, and you won't have time for any of the things you need to do to keep yourself sane and balanced. You always work too much. If you get a day job, there won't be any way to control the hours. Someone else will be in charge.

Me: What would help?

Jellyfish: Don't work for anyone else. You need to make a day job for yourself so you can control the hours.

Me: Okay. I can do that. Anything else you want me to know?

Jellyfish: Making a day job for yourself is doable. You show other people how to do it all the time.

Me: Thanks for the input.

Next, the Judge and Me

Me: Judge, what concerns do you have about me making or getting a day job?

Judge: That you'll find something awful, and you'll just stay with it because you'll get stuck. I'm afraid there's no decent job out there for you. [Note: my Judge is right. I tend to get stuck in situations that aren't helpful for me].

Me: What would help?

Judge: Promise you won't do anything awful.

Me: I promise. Anything else you want me to know?

Judge: No—just keep your promise that you won't sign up to do stuff you hate, then stay there forever.

Me: Done.

Now, a Conversation With the Jailer

Me: Jailer—what are your concerns about me making or getting a day job?

Jailer: I'm afraid you'll actually figure out something and succeed. Then you'll start showing your writing. And then the criticism will start.

Me: That might happen. Glad you think I might succeed. That makes me feel good. How can I help mitigate your fear?

Jailer: You can't. That's just what's going to happen.

Me: I know you're afraid I'll be criticized. But there's no way around it. I'll be critical of myself if I don't try.

Jailer: Visibility is just so dangerous for you.

Me: It is, I guess. We could ignore the haters.

Jailer: It's the silence that's worse.

Me: I'm confused. You think I'll succeed, but you're worried more about silence and no attention?

Jailer: I'm worried about all of it.

Me: Okay. We can start small. What if I define success in a modest way and see if I can achieve that first?

Jailer: Okay. That would work. Thank you.

Me: Anything else you want me to know?

Jailer: Defining success makes me feel calmer. Please do that.

Me: I will.

My Safety Squad is asking me for some specific, and in this case, reasonable actions. Sometimes their requests are unreasonable ("Don't finish this book," for instance.) They can sometimes be loud and uncooperative, especially at the beginning of peace talks.

You're on to Them Now

When you feel resistance and fear, you know what's going on and what to do about it. You go from being the victim to being the boss. You get to decide whether to thank them for sharing, going in the direction you feel is best, or listening to what they want and granting their requests.

In my case, the requests are reasonable. My Jellyfish wants to make sure I don't exhaust myself. My Judge wants me to avoid landing in a toxic situation I won't leave. My Jailer is asking for something more concrete. It's requesting I define success with my art (in my case, my books) modestly. There's history behind this request.

In the past I've defined success by one measurement: did I get on the New York *Times* bestseller list? I felt shame when the answer was no. I could define success by looking at the number of people my books have influenced; how many creative people are getting their art into the world because of my work; or how many people I've helped, rather than using an abstract, external measurement which doesn't mean much ***and*** makes me feel miserable. Defining success modestly like this is a perceptive suggestion, and I will take it.

"Let the beauty
of what you love
be what you do."
~ Rumi

The Beginnings of Helpful Advice

This conversation and the requests by the Safety Squad are examples of helpful advice. I'm still the boss (so are you), but you may find they offer useful counsel once they know you'll hear them out, counsel you might decide to take.

Anytime you feel yourself getting anxious; while reading this chapter or when taking steps to make your financial life more peaceful, it's likely one or more of the Safety Squad is activated. Stop and talk to them. This will reduce and sometimes remove the fear altogether, and you might get some useful advice.

Now for the Practical Side of a Day Job

Let's look at what you need to do to get or make a day job.

Step one is to determine how much money you require to live peacefully, so you know what your day job needs to generate.

There are at least a hundred books on financial planning that will teach you how much you need to earn and save. I want to be kind to you and your Safety Squad, so we're going to take it slowly and make this, dare I say, maybe even fun. Or at least interesting. So, rather than consulting those books or haranguing you about spending and saving and blah blah blah, I'm going to teach you a trick. The quick and dirty way to figure out how much money you need to live on is to add up everything you've spent over the last three months and divide it by three. (You can probably download all your spending from your bank to get the number).

Yes, this is just a crude estimate. I want to keep the estimation process ultra-simple. I don't want to remobilize your Safety Squad by making this complex and tedious. Start with this number. You can revise it as you go along.

Write your number here: ______________________.

Now you know how much money you need from your day job.

There Are Five Simple Paths to a Day Job

Path # 1. First, and most obvious, work for someone else. Here's what to watch for if you choose this path.

The perfect day job is twenty to thirty hours a week and stimulates a different part of the brain used to create. It pays all your bills, includes health insurance, and leaves your creative mind free and your body relaxed enough to do your art.

A few words of caution about this path: First, if you can, stay away from jobs that traditionally require long hours. Technology jobs and selling cars can be demanding this way.

Second, try not to get a job that is sort of like doing your art, but imposes constraints on your creativity to the point that you might feel like you're trying to do art in prison.

Take a day job like graphic design, which is clearly creative and artistic. Some painters and other 2D artists can handle it, maybe even went to school for it. But for others, being a graphic designer often places them in a position where they must listen to and heed someone with no design skills. If you can handle that, or you're interested in helping people learn how to trust your design skills, great. If not, stay away. Any type of technical or marketing writing might suck the lifeblood of a writer. Construction work might be tough for sculptors.

You'll know. If the thought of the job makes you sick to your stomach, that's your sign to keep looking.

In addition to money, what other needs could a day job meet? If you're mostly alone when you do your art, maybe you need a day job where you're around people. If your art is sedentary (like writing), maybe your day job needs to involve some physical activity. A cartoonist once told me he loved the assembly line day job he worked in his twenties. His hands were occupied but the job didn't require much intellectual exertion, so he was able to work out story lines in his head while he earned money to pay his bills.

I once read an article about a famous writer whose day job was teaching writing at Stanford University. The person who wrote the article wondered if the famous writer would have been more prolific if he hadn't been 'forced' to work at a day job.

I think it's possible he would have written less. I don't know if you can do your art eight hours a day. I can't. Four hours is my maximum, and 30-minute sessions work even better. I need to do other tasks the rest of the time so my unconscious can labor over the next day's writing without my interference. Why not get paid to work at your day job while your Muse is coming up with new ideas for the next day's art?

Path #2. Teach. Lots of creatives teach in public and private schools, or are adjuncts or full-time teachers in college. Another option is to substitute. Having someone else find your students for you and pay you to teach them can be an easy way to go, or you can gather your own students and turn that into your day job.

Teaching doesn't have to mean working just with kids or beginners, either. Your fellow musicians, painters, sculptors, dancers and singers might like to take master classes from you. Look around at other creatives in your field who also teach. They can be a great source of inspiration.

There are a lot of platforms already in place you can plug into to help you find students. Right now, Thumbtack.com, Udemy.com, Skillshare.com, and Teachable.com are possibilities, but do your research before you commit to one. No telling what's sprung up since I hit 'send' to upload this book for publication. Powerful tools like Zoom and WebEx and GoToMeeting make holding everything from online one-on-one sessions to large webinars fairly simple. Do your research here too. The challenge isn't the teaching itself; it's finding the right students. The chapter on finding your people will help if you choose this route.

Path #3. Is someone paying you to do something already? Do you enjoy it? Can you see a way to get more of this work, either from the same people or from others? Could you meet your needs doing this work without having to devote fifty hours a week to it? If you're already getting paid to do something you enjoy and you can see a way to get more of this work, start there.

The best example for this situation (and the one that follows) is to help other people with their social media. If you're already on social media and you like it, this might be a place to look to make yourself a day job. Writers might be good Twitter account managers; visual artists could run Instagram feeds. The reason I'm suggesting doing social media for other people is because of your gift; your creativity. It can turn someone's mundane social media presence into something worth following.

Path #4. Do you do something well that someone would pay for? Even if no one is paying you for it yet (see social media example above), look around at the tasks you can do with your eyes closed. People often think, "No one would pay me to do that. It's too simple." This is a common fallacy. You might not be able to conceive that others struggle with a task you can do easily. I guarantee people are looking for someone to do what you do well because it baffles them. I personally can't do administrative work. I feel guilty about this, but I finally realized my weaknesses are job descriptions for other people. What comes naturally to you, that bedevils other people, and could that be your day job?

Path #5 is to turn an aspect of your art into a day job. If you are willing to collaborate, adapt your art, or turn to your clients for direct support, your art might provide a path to a sustainable day job. Because of the internet there are now a myriad of ways to do this, which is why this idea merits a whole chapter on its own.

Photo by Matthew Lejune on Unsplash

SEVEN

Crazes and Commissions

MODIFY YOUR ART FOR FUN AND PROFIT.

There are three approaches to modifying parts of your art to make a day job with it.

The first is to collaborate with other people. This could mean commissions, joint projects, or partnerships. The second is to adapt aspects of your art by changing the media, venue, form, or other characteristics of it to make it more accessible to more people. The third is to work with your clients to see what additional products or services they might need or want from you that you would be willing to provide.

Let's Look at Collaboration First

Collaboration is simply taking input from another person, or group of people, that results in your making something different (not cheapened or diminished, just different) than what you'd make on your own. The classic collaboration is a commission.

Theoretically, people commission you to do or make or compose or write something because they like your style and wouldn't want you to change anything, but of course, that's not always true. A commission ends up being a collaboration between artist and buyer.

One client I worked with collaborates with city governments and developers to create large-scale murals in public spaces. She conceives the original designs which are reviewed by a committee. They rarely question her plans, but they can, and sometimes do. She listens to her gut when they ask for revisions; changes her design when her gut gives her the green light, and says no if it doesn't. As she is selected to create more and more projects for more cities, her credibility increases. The committees begin to trust her artistic judgment more and ask for revisions less.

Many cities around the world have budgets for public art of all kinds, and to work with governmental entities like these, no matter where they are, you have to learn how to collaborate and know when to compromise.

Real estate developers often want to add public art to their developments. Choirs and orchestras and couples getting married commission music from composers. People commission paintings for their homes and offices or portraits of their children and dogs. Dance companies commission pieces from choreographers. Cities commission public art from sculptors, painters, and musicians. Theater companies commission plays from playwrights. All these collaborations are legitimate ways for artists to get their work into the world and get paid for it.

Another way to collaborate is to find an artist whose work you admire and complements yours and do a joint project. Then you can each tell the people who follow you about the collaboration, magnifying your audience reach. Painters and photographers collaborate like this frequently; a painter will make something, the photographer will shoot it, then each one can tell their people about the results of the collaboration.

The obvious collaborations many artists, musicians, and writers often long for is to find a gallery, a music label or a publisher; a gatekeeper, to collaborate with. In this perfect world, the gatekeeper finds your work, loves it, has a ready market for it, and assumes the responsibility for getting it into the world, selling it, collecting the money, then paying you. The good news, in theory, is a collaboration like this frees you to simply do your art, while someone else handles the business and money.

The Bad News Comes in Two Forms

First, most gatekeepers are only willing to take on artists who already have a following. This is certainly true in the publishing business. Publishers want writers to have a 'platform,' that is a sizeable group of people already interested in the writer's work, before they agree to publish a book by someone unknown. If you must have a following before a gatekeeper takes you on, why not just continue to build your following, and interact with your people directly?

Second, there can be an imbalance of power, in that, 'She who has the gold makes the rules.' If you abdicate the responsibility for getting your art into the world to someone else, they will have the right to ask for a lot of input about what you're making. Just like any business, the department that makes the product often clashes with the people who sell it. The best design isn't always the easiest to sell, and the easiest thing to sell isn't always the best design. It may be simpler to work through that conflict if you're trying to reconcile it within yourself.

Getting a gatekeeper to choose you used to be the only way to get your work into the world. That's not true anymore. Go ahead and pitch them if you want; just know the internet provides the choice if you decide to pick yourself.

Does Your Art Lend Itself to Collaboration?

If so, what would it look like for you? If you can find the boundary between collaboration and unacceptable compromise and stay on the right side of the line, you can make a day job out of collaboration.

Could You Adapt Your Art?

The second way to make a day job from your art is to adapt it. If you're a 2D or 3D artist you can adapt your subject matter. You could choose a specific subject the way photographers shoot landscapes for people to buy as souvenirs to remind them of beautiful places. A painter I worked with adapts her subject matter by making drawings, prints and paintings of her hometown, Cleveland, Ohio. Like many cities, Cleveland is the home of striking, iconic architecture. Her clients who live there enjoy displaying her prints of these landmarks in their homes and offices. She is willing to dedicate some of her creativity and time to this single subject to make a day job from it, and there is already a market for souvenirs of Cleveland.

You could adapt your art by making some of it functional. You can print images on almost anything, from mugs to wallpaper to clothing, fabric, dishes, pillows and scarves. The advantage of this is two-fold: printing images on functional items will give your people a wider range of work to buy from you at different prices, and all these items can be printed on demand, so you never need to buy and hold inventory.

The downside is that you have to sell a lot of mugs to make any money. There are several internet-based companies that will help you upload your images to print them on virtually anything, but do your research and don't expect that once you've uploaded your designs you can sit back and watch the money roll in. You will be competing with thousands if not millions of other sellers on these sites. You'll still be responsible to find your people and help them buy from you. Every site has a different pricing policy also. Make sure you understand what percentage of the sale you earn, and how long it takes them to pay you, along with how good their customer service is. You don't want them alienating your people.

Another way to adapt your art is making copies of your originals; prints of your paintings, replicas of your sculptures, recordings of your live performances.

Adapt Your Art to a Current Trend

Two trends burning through North America right now are choosing a word of the year for yourself and buying customized face masks to protect you from the current pandemic. My book coach who is also a fine artist, makes mandalas from words. You can buy a mandala from her that contains your personal word of the year. Depending on your art you could take advantage of this trend where demand for products already exists by writing a song incorporating someone's word of the year, making a piece of jewelry, a painting, or a print.

Artists are also printing images of their photography, paintings, drawings and designs on masks. Demand for masks has risen exponentially over the last year and may be around a long time. You could decide to adapt your work to this or any number of current trends.

Similarly, you can also fit your art to a market that already exists. Souvenirs fit into this category. There is already a market for objects that remind people of their visits to extraordinary places.

The rituals of our lives also have an existing market: every holiday, birthday, marriage and divorce, graduation, adoption, even death, all trigger purchases to mark them. Could your art be adapted to commemorate one of these milestones?

“An artist is not
paid for his labor
but for his vision.”
~ James McNeill Whistler

There are probably other ways to adapt your art that I haven't thought of. Go online where artists hang out and see what they're doing and whether any of their ideas would work for you.

Do Your People Want More From You?

The third way to turn your art into a day job is to see what else the people who buy from you might need that's related to your art, and supply it to them.

This will require you to figure out who your people are. That's next after you talk to the Creative Council and the Safety Squad in the next chapter. Once you get acquainted with your people you might discover they need more help related to the art you're already making, or they might want to interact with you directly, or both. Here are examples.

One of the painters whose work I bought, suggested I hire her to help me arrange and hang all my other paintings and artwork, in addition to hers. I was happy to hire her for this service, since I have no eye for composition. I ended up with two new paintings plus all of the artwork I already owned being arranged and hung in my home in a way I could never have accomplished on my own. She created a mini gallery for me. This is an example of additional work I wanted, needed, and was willing to pay for, in addition to buying the paintings themselves.

Your people might also want to interact with you directly. They might want to know what you admire, what you listen to, what you read, and what you think is important. This is sometimes called your brand.

Don't Scream Yet

Before you start screaming at me that turning yourself into a brand will utterly corrupt your creativity and transform you into a money-grubbing egomaniac, let me suggest something that might surprise you.

Unless you have no friends, no family, and you've shown your work to no one, you already are a brand to people. Your brand is simply your personality, a description of who you are in the world. How you carry yourself, what you decide to make, what your work looks like, sounds like, or acts like, is establishing your brand.

Because you've spent time honing your craft, your eye for good design, your ear for music, or a poetic sentence, your body for expressive dance, or whatever your art is, you have something valuable to share with other people. In addition to your art itself, you have expertise, knowledge, and experience that many others don't have.

Maybe you provide a window into your design sensibility, your curatorial skills, or aesthetic sense. Maybe other artists want to learn from you (see "Teaching" as a possible day job). Maybe your people want to go on trips to the theatre districts in Manhattan or London (or virtually), where you select the plays, teach what to look for, and give them a behind-the scenes look at what it takes to mount a production. Or you create writers' retreats, a series of instructional videos on how to play the guitar, or how to draw.

If making yourself into a more public figure disturbs you, don't do it. But if you can see yourself interacting with your people this way, there are thousands of examples of other artists doing this. Currently you can find them on Instagram and Pinterest, perhaps Facebook, Clubhouse, or TikTok. Do your research to see where artists like you hang out.

Then There's Old-Fashioned Patronage

You can also interact with your people by asking them if they would be willing to support you with small monthly or yearly donations, or fund specific projects. Many people want to support creatives and are willing to donate. Patreon and Buy Me A Coffee are two sites that facilitate donations. There are also crowdfunding sites like Indiegogo, GoFundMe and Kickstarter that can help you fund specific projects. In any case, do your research.

The Safety Squad, particularly the Judge and Jailer, will probably become agitated by the idea of being a brand or asking your people to sustain you with donations or to fund new work. The Judge may say something along the lines of "Who do you think you are asking for someone to pay you just because you're you?" The Jailer won't like how visible you'll become if you consider making yourself a brand. You might need to listen to the Safety Squad's concerns before you start down either of these roads. Becoming a brand or asking for patronage can be two of the scariest actions artists can take. Your Safety Squad will probably get extremely loud. Listen to their concerns but remember that you are the boss.

For your own sanity, you'll need to preserve time and energy for your pure artistic practice while you decide whether some aspect of your art could be a day job. I can tell which artists I've worked with aren't doing that when I first meet them. I sometimes joke that artists not doing their art are cranky, but the deeper truth is they feel grief-stricken and debilitated when their pure art doesn't have a voice or place in the world. Handle this first.

Once your artistic expression is secure, you can look at your whole practice and see if some part of it can be made into a day job that can provide a stable financial foundation for your life.

Photo by Austin Chan on Unsplash

EIGHT

Seeking Guidance

YODA, THE RISK MANAGEMENT DEPARTMENT, AND YOU.

Let's start this process of making or getting a day job by talking to your Mentor.

This may seem radical or strange, especially if you feel like you have no idea where to start to make yourself a day job. But try having this conversation with your Mentor anyway to see if she knows what your day job might look like. No pressure. Just see what shows up. Here is a list of possible questions. As usual, follow the conversation as it unfolds and ask follow-up or different questions that occur to you as you listen.

Questions for Your Mentor About Your Day Job

What could my day job look like?

What should I sell/make/do?

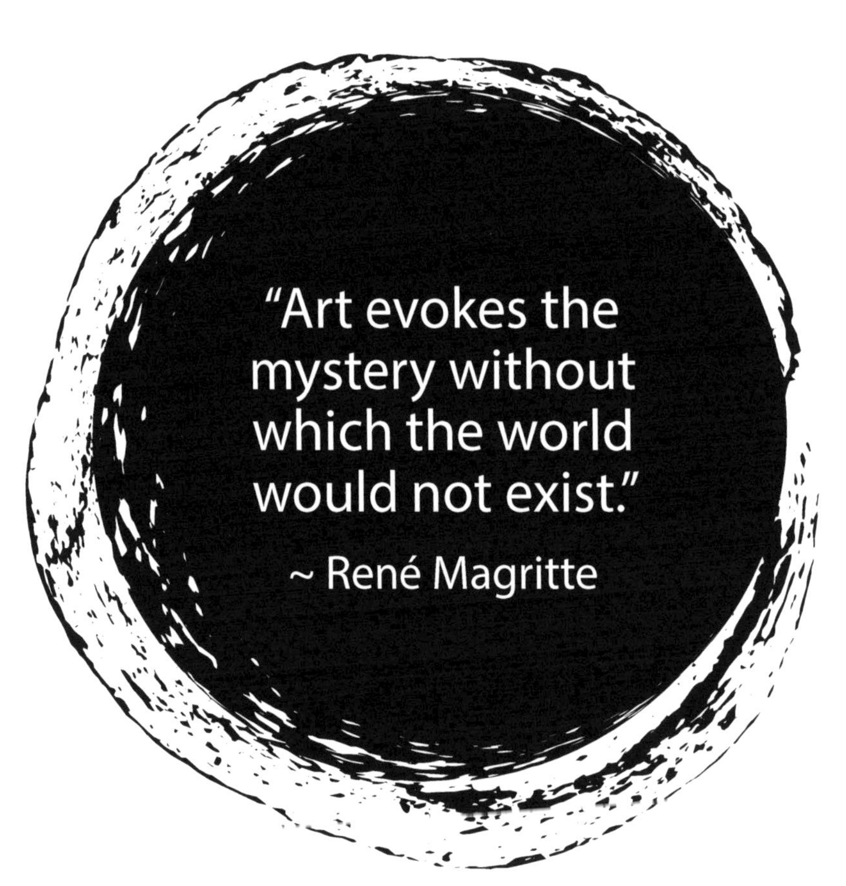
"Art evokes the mystery without which the world would not exist."
~ René Magritte

Who are my best clients/customers?

Where can I find them?

What should I say to them?

Am I already doing something I could make into a day job?

Where should I start/what should I do first?

What other advice do you have for me?

Next, let's see if any of the Safety Squad would like to weigh in on your day job. Ask if any of them want to step forward and answer any of these questions.

How do you feel about me making or getting a day job?

What advice do you have about me doing this?

How should I get started?

What should I watch out for?

Are there things I should do to stay safe?

Anything else you want me to know?

Whether you work for someone else or make a day job for yourself, you'll begin to notice that your scarce resource won't be money anymore. It'll be time. Making sure there's time for everything, including your art, is next.

Photo by Liz Wiltzen, PCC, CPCC, Coach, Writer, Artist

NINE

Rocks in Jars

TIME MANAGEMENT FOR ARTISTS (AND GEOLOGISTS).

Making time for your art is challenging, necessary, maybe even crucial. You've probably struggled with this already, and the clamoring of your Safety Squad is the primary reason for the struggle. As we covered previously, making sure you don't have time for your art, so you never create anything, is an efficient scheme your Safety Squad concocted to keep you safe.

Rather than harangue you about "managing" your time better, I'm going to tell you a story and give you some tools to reassure the Safety Squad.

Stephen Covey, a bestselling author who wrote about leadership, tells this story in one of his books.

A philosophy professor puts a glass jar on his desk and fills it with large rocks. He asks his students, "Is the jar full?" They fall for the trick question and say, "Yes." He then takes a handful or two of smaller pebbles and pours them into the jar. They fall into the spaces between the large rocks, and they fit. He asks again, "Is the jar full?" The students, not catching on, say, "Yes, this time it's full." The professor then takes out some sand and pours that into the jar. It fits also.

The Students Finaly Get the Point

This is a time management analogy. The big rocks represent the work in your life that is most important. When you put that in the jar first, you can fit the less important stuff (the pebbles, then the sand) around the big rocks. But if you go about this the opposite way; if you fill your days with the sand, the fluff, the unimportant, there's never room for the rocks.

The rocks are the things in your life you value highly, like love, art, self-care, spirituality, family, everything brings you meaning and joy.

Yes, Your Art Is One of the Big Rocks

You probably recognize intuitively that your art belongs in the jar with all the other priceless activities of your life. But even if you don't, if you haven't placed your art in that category before, I hope you will now.

Here's why. If I've been successful at imparting one piece of information to you thus far, it's that your work matters. It matters a lot. And things that matter a lot need you to give them time regularly and if possible, generously.

You'll Gain Two Rewards

First, when you dedicate regular, frequent time to your art you'll get better. Musicians know this beneficial cycle intimately. More practice, get better, enjoy playing more, practice more, get better.... Second, weirdly and miraculously, once you consciously dedicate time to your art and to the other essential activities in your life, time seems to appear to handle the less important stuff too. For some reason, it never works the other way around.

When Are You Most Creative?

Once you decide to dedicate regular time to your art, you'll need to understand when you are the most alert and connected to your creativity. Just like personal financial management, there are innumerable books about time management to help you figure this out. You could buy one. But I'm guessing you already know the answer.

It's not so hard to notice when you are most creatively productive. The tricky part is handling the Safety Squad's objections that will inevitably arise when you try setting aside the time.

But let's not take a chance. In case you're unclear about when your most creative times are during the day, there's a source for that information.

Your Maker Knows

Your Maker: the part of your brain that knows your craft, that knows how to make your art, may also know when to make it. Let's ask. I've suggested some questions for you to start the conversation with your Maker below.

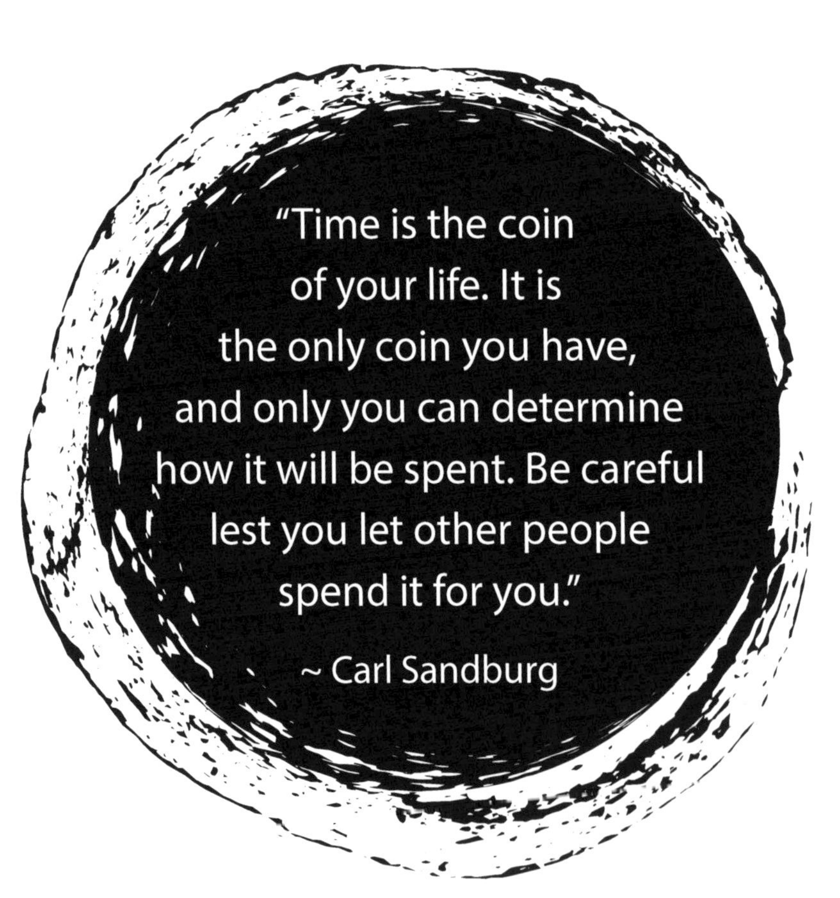

"Time is the coin
of your life. It is
the only coin you have,
and only you can determine
how it will be spent. Be careful
lest you let other people
spend it for you."
~ Carl Sandburg

Questions for Your Maker

What times would be best for me to do art?

Any advice about how to make sure I set aside this time?

What should I say to family/friends about this time?

What should I do if I'm not in the mood?

Anything else you want me to know or do?

If you already know when your most creative times are, but you can't seem to make yourself sit down and work during those times, then someone in the Safety Squad is active. Find out which one is blocking you here.

Questions for the Safety Squad

Which Safety Squad member is worried about me setting aside time for my art?

(It's possible one, two or all three members are resisting your blocking out regular time to do your art. If so, have this conversation with each one that's resisting.)

What worries you about me setting aside regular time to do my art?

What are you protecting me from?

How can we cooperate?

Anything else you want me to know?

I Understand That You Have Significant Life Responsibilities Besides Your Art

They might be so demanding that you can only set aside an hour or less a day for your creative practice. You're not alone. I wasn't exaggerating when I said that whole books get written by authors writing fifteen minutes a day. You can buy books that show you exactly how to do it. A painter whose stunning work I have hanging in my living room, finishes a lot of work painting 45 minutes a day.

Don't Let the Lack of Time Deter You

An hour, 45 minutes, or even 15 minutes a day is infinitely better than no minutes. Where you start and how much time you allocate is much less important than the starting itself and the sticking with it.

"Where the
spirit does not work
with the hand,
there is no art."
~ Leonardo da Vinci

Photo by Shane Rounce on Unsplash

TEN

You Have People

IT'S

DESTINY.

If you've decided you want your art to make joy for you and others, as well as making money, the next step is to figure out who your people are and where to find them.

This means that you will have to face a couple of the horsemen of the apocalypse: marketing and sales. But before you and the Safety Squad all run screaming, let me show you a way to look at marketing and selling with a different set of eyes.

Marketing and Selling Aren't Legal Forms of Prostitution

But right now, you might secretly feel that way about them. We've all been bombarded by advertising (which is just one type of marketing) about products that promised far more than they delivered. In fact, there's even a word for marketing that borders on lying but doesn't cross over; it's called puffery. You could be forgiven for not wanting to have anything to do with any of this, especially in the context of your precious art.

Next, the idea that people need and want your art, and ***you can figure out who these people are,*** might seem implausible. You may hear a member of the Squad say something along the lines of: "Are you telling me that my art has a 'target market' just like dental floss or socks? That I should 'sell' my art the way Ford sells cars?"

The short answers are yes and yes. Your art does have a target market; by that I mean there are people who need and want your art, and these people have certain characteristics in common. Plus, once you know something about your people, who they are, where they hang out, where they expect to find you; you can find ***them*** and start making actual human relationships.

This is the shift I'm asking you to consider: the shift from viewing marketing and selling as a contest to see who can tell the biggest lies, to viewing it as a way to find the people who want your art and to make real relationships with them.

The first step in this process is to figure out who needs and wants your art. You'll do that by having a conversation with your Mentor.

Why Your Mentor?

Because the most effective marketing that leads to the most sales (and the most repeat sales) is marketing that communicates the purpose of your art. That shows your people they need what you make. And your Mentor knows your purpose.

The Safety Squad Might Scream and the Jailer Might Be Loudest

All three members of the Safety Squad may worry about you finding your people, but the one most likely to rebel the fiercest at the prospect of finding them is the Jailer. Since the Jailer's job is to hide you and your art from the outside world, the idea that people need and want your art, then deciding to find those people, is the opposite of hiding. The Jailer will most likely point out you've already suffered some pain when you've invited other people to experience your art and it will be right. Virtually no artist escapes criticism from someone who matters to them. If the Jailer is really troubled or strident, have a conversation and ask what it needs to feel safe.

In the Meantime, Start Here

First, you'll need to know some specific information about your people so you can find them. Here's a list of the information you need.

1. Who are they objectively? What is their age, sex, location, marital status, number of children, their level of education? This is demographic information; factual data that the U.S. and other governments around the world collect when they take a census.

2. Who are they personally? What do they care about? What are their political, spiritual, emotional beliefs? What do they value and what do they not? This is called psychographic information. Describe your people's personalities, world view and beliefs. Who are they as people, aside from their external characteristics?

3. If you already have customers, how did they come to you? Did someone refer them, or did you start a conversation on Pinterest or Instagram or Myspace (kidding) or did you teach a class where they met you? Did you meet them at a concert or a charity event?

"I want to touch
people with my art."
~ Vincent Van Gogh

If you already have customers for your art and you enjoy working with them, you can skip to the next chapter and fill in the information about them right now.

If you don't have any customers for your art yet and you want to see what a sample conversation might look like with your Mentor, read on.

Inspiration From the Mentor

This is an edited conversation I had with my Mentor about my people (that's you!). Your conversation may resemble this, or it may be completely different. Experiment in the next chapter and see what emerges.

C: Hi. May I talk to my Mentor about who wants and needs my art?

M: Sure.

C: Who are they on the outside (age, sex, sexual orientation, kids, etc.)?

M: They're in their 30's and 40's. Maybe early 50's. They still have a lot of juice for their art. It's not a hobby. They need to know you accept everyone regardless of their sexual orientation or gender. They aren't conventional or judgmental and they need you to be that way too. They live mostly in urban areas. Downtowns. Funky places... not the ticky-tacky suburbs. Can't stand that. They include their kids in their creativity. Their kids inspire them. They went to college. Education is not their problem. They have day jobs. They make okay money. Not tons. They have no debt. Stuff doesn't matter to them. They can make a funky wardrobe from a thrift store and an eccentric and beautiful home from Goodwill stuff. They care about issues but don't give a crap about which party champions them. Health insurance is somewhat of a problem. They put it

out of their minds if their day job provides it, but they aren't sure how they'd afford it if they went out on their own.

C: Who are they on the inside?

M: They care about honoring the creative force inside them. They feel like they're carrying around a precious child or priceless motivation that they have to listen to and respect and obey as much as they can, or it will disappear or maybe even die. They care about family and friends, of course, but the family and friends don't necessarily understand this force inside them. This force or motivation or genius or whatever it is has picked them to manifest it into the world and they feel required to do that. Not only will it disappear if they don't, but if they don't help it come into the world, it will be harmful to them. They are motivated to get their art into the world, but don't know where to start, or if they should even try. But it's bugging them to work in obscurity. They need you to keep them in reality. Help them translate what they're doing into words so they can talk about it. They need you to help them stay grounded, not stuck in their feelings. They start criticizing themselves and can't work or barely even function when that happens. You told someone you were a backstop for creative people. That's what they need. They need you to remind them what they're up to, why they're doing it, and what they need to do to reach their own people, with a minimum of self-criticism or fear.

C: What do they need from me?

M: Some step-by-step stuff on Instagram so they can start small without you. They're pretty battered by all the crap this culture slings at them, so make their first steps super easy and small. Videos are good too. Put links on Instagram and on your website. Keep the videos short.

C: Anything else?

M: Look hard at the stuff you want them to do and chop it into 5-minute chunks. Seriously, this will help you clarify and simplify what you're doing also.

C: Okay. Thank you. This has been really helpful.

Experimentation Is Your Friend

Identifying your people may involve a lot of experimentation. I've been experimenting with figuring out who my people are and how to find and talk to them for at least fifteen years. As your creative practice changes, your people might change too, or you might have two or three different sets of people depending on what you're making. I try to view the whole process as one giant, interesting, evolving experiment.

Here Comes the Judge

When you start talking to your Mentor about your people, the Judge may become agitated again. You might hear something along the lines of "This is stupid," or "How do you expect talking to an imaginary person is going to help you figure out who to sell your art to?" (Hmm…maybe the Judge forgot that it is also imaginary.)

The answer to this objection is this: you have to start somewhere. Talking to your Mentor taps into a part of your brain that has some ideas about who your clients are and how to start making relationships with them. As you start talking to your people in real life, you'll better understand them and can refine your messages accordingly.

Now Let's Have That Chat with Your Mentor

Whether you already have clients for your art or not, before you talk to your Mentor about them, envision and feel the people you most want to see, hear, experience, and possess your art. Who will cry or rejoice at your concerts? Who will be delighted, inspired, or motivated by your art? Who will stay awake until 3 a.m. reading your books?

Start your conversation with the Mentor by asking these questions, but if others occur to you, ask them.

Questions for the Mentor

Who are my people on the outside (age/race/sex/education/location/income level)?

Who are my people on the inside (what are their spiritual/political/cultural beliefs)?

What matters most to them?

Who are they as people?

What problems do they face that my art might help with?

What do they need from me?

Why do they need this?

Anything else you want me to know?

After you find out who they are, the next set of questions dig deeper into what they want from you.

What situation or problem in their life do they want my art to change for them?

How will my art help change the situation or their feelings about it?

What is important about changing this situation?

How do they feel about the situation now?

How do they want to feel after they buy my art?

Do they have any fears about buying my art? If so, what are they?

Anything else?

Art Evokes Emotion

This is your marketing—helping people understand your art will provide experiences and help them feel the emotions they crave. In the next chapter you'll practice talking about the emotions that your art evokes, so your people can recognize your art is what they're looking for.

Photo by Kristopher Roller on Unsplash

ELEVEN

Now Go Find Them

WHERE ARE THEY, WHO ARE THEY, WHAT DO THEY NEED?

As I shared in the day job chapter, if your work was judged first-rate by a gatekeeper a gallery owner, record label, publisher, promoter, editor, or agent, you'd be chosen by them, and they would handle all the dirty stuff; marketing, promotion, publicity, and best of all, the selling. You'd be left in peaceful bliss to do your art and cash your checks.

This did happen for a tiny, well-connected, mostly white, often male sliver of the population. Most creatives never broke into this artistic nirvana. Before the internet, most creatives toiled in obscurity. The chances of some promoter hearing you play at your local bar, or an editor picking your book out of a slush pile were virtually nil.

The internet has changed all this for the better. We're in a golden age for artists. No one stands between you and your people anymore. There are masses of simple, inexpensive, even free tools to make finding your people, making relationships, and helping them buy straightforward, if not effortless.

What Could Go Wrong?

You probably already know, because you've experienced it. Just like knowing second grade math, the level of math skill needed to handle money, doesn't erase the fear about it, having simple, inexpensive tools to help you find and make relationships with your people doesn't erase (or even address) the fear of re-experiencing the trauma that seems to be an inevitable part of letting people see your art. This is the Safety Squad, especially the Jailer's, home turf.

Signs My Jailer Was Already Hard at Work

The Jailer may already be working its immobilizing magic behind the scenes without you even knowing. My Jailer helped me create a bunch of clutter, both in my office and on my computer. I wasted hours looking for things and rearranging the piles. I was inconsistent in maintaining relationships with my people, and my Jailer, with my full cooperation, came up with plausible excuses for why this was okay.

I didn't wake up in the morning aware that I was afraid of being visible. The Jailer was my silent partner in creating enough problems for me that becoming visible was simply impossible.

Is Your Jailer Also Working Overtime?

Maybe you've got a convincing reason why you aren't technical enough to make a website for yourself, or you don't want your privacy invaded so you won't post on social media (like one photographer client who made his Instagram account private, then took it one step further and turned down everyone who asked to follow him). Maybe you pack your schedule with perfectly legitimate activities, so you never have time to market. Or, perhaps when people inquire about buying something, you forget to respond to them because you're too busy, disorganized, or preoccupied.

Or maybe what's actually happening is the Jailer is working overtime to keep you in jail too.

Does any of this sound familiar? If you feel worried or troubled by the idea of finding the people who need your art and making relationships with them, it's probably the Jailer at work. If so, there are two ways to make peace so you can move forward.

The first is to talk to the Jailer the way you did in the Peace Talks chapter, where you communicated with each member of the Safety Squad. You can ask additional questions, such as, "What do you protect me from? What are you afraid will happen to me? What do you want me to know?" You know now the Jailer is on your side, trying to prevent you from experiencing more trauma.

A Counterintuitive Proposal

The other way to calm the Jailer, or any other member of the Safety Squad trying to prevent you from finding your people, is to slowly start doing your marketing. This probably sounds counterintuitive. It works because as you start marketing, you'll begin to meet the people who need you. Knowing them will remind you why you're doing what you do, which stimulates your creativity. You'll make more and better work which will fuel your desire to reach more people, and suddenly you're on the road. This is the performing artists' original virtuous cycle, and it works for all artists. An appreciative audience inspires you to want to perform better, more often, in front of even more people.

"Art should be
something that
liberates your soul,
provokes the imagination
and encourages people
to go further."
~ Keith Haring

What Is This Marketing Stuff I'm Talking About?

What am I talking about here? What is "your marketing," anyway? I've alluded to it already. It's a three-step process: finding your people, making relationships with them, and helping them buy. Here's the magic formula.

1. Get a website and put your best work there.
2. Figure out which social media sites your people are likely to visit, and open accounts. Find your people on these sites and interact with them regularly. Focus your effort on pointing them to your website, where they can opt-in with their email address and hear from you personally.
3. Talk weekly to the people who opted in and gave you permission. Talk about what you're working on, what inspires you, your creative process, other people you admire. Offer helpful insights and information. Austin Kleon wrote a simple book about how to do this, called *Show Your Work*.
4. Make it easy for your people to buy from you on your website with clear descriptions, prices and streamlined ordering.

That's it.

Why Can't I Just Put Up a _______ (Fill in the Blank) Social Media Page?

Why am I telling you to put up a website, when you can open an account on Facebook or Instagram or LinkedIn or Twitter or Pinterest (or some other social media site we don't yet know about) for free and sell from there? Two reasons. First, social media connections are ephemeral and flimsy. Your followers make no commitment to you beyond the virtually effortless clicking on the 'Follow' or 'Like' button. Second, and more important, the site controls your data, not you. They can decide to do whatever they want with it, and they will.

Social media's superpower is that it provides a place to find and begin interacting with people you couldn't find otherwise. It's like a giant cocktail party or the world's largest perpetual networking event. It's a place to meet new people. Once you meet them, though, you want to deepen the relationship by asking their permission to stay in touch with them through your website. The committed, interested ones (the ones you want) will say yes.

What If I Believe Social Media Is Breaking the Culture?

There is a case to be made that social media is the work of the devil and you should stay away from it. Their algorithms funnel us into sites that confirm our biases, inflame our emotions and narrow our world view. These critiques are true, and some artists have opted out of social media altogether because of this. If you feel like this, you can certainly focus your efforts to help your people find you in other ways. Social media is just the easiest.

If you are morally opposed to supporting the social media juggernaut (or just don't want to be there), attend or create events where your people would hang out, find other artists and cooperate with them to get exposure to people you don't know. Network with your people or find them in other ways. But no matter what you do, direct everyone to your website, and be sure there's a place on each page for people to opt in to get your updates.

Next, Let's Make Friends

Once you've established your presence so your people can find you, let's talk about how to make relationships with them.

Starting the Conversation

The best way to start any relationship is to share things about yourself. Luckily, you're in possession of your glamorous, fascinating, artistic life, and people are genuinely interested in what that looks like. You could spend the rest of your days just showing your creative process and your work in progress, sharing what inspires and spurs you to action, talking about how you overcome blocks, or discussing select details of your daily life, especially the ways all these activities fuel your purpose and your art. Information about your activities that might seem mundane to you will charm and enthrall your people. Just start sharing your process regularly and revise what you share based on the feedback you receive.

What's Next?

The way to create a plan to be visible, find your people and make relationships with them, is to have a conversation with the Mentor, who will have ideas about where your people want to find you and what they want to know about you. Then we'll talk to the Jailer who's the most likely Safety Squad member to be worried about what happens when you start being found.

Questions for Your Mentor

Where do my people want to find me? Website, social media, (which platform), in person (where), other ideas?

What do my people want to see/read/feel when they find me?

What shall I write about, or photograph, or make videos of?

How do they want me to help them buy?

Anything else you want me to know?

Next, let's talk to the Jailer about visibility.

Here are some possible questions:

How do you feel about me being visible?

What can I do to alleviate your concerns?

How can we work together?

Is there anything else you want me to know?

The Most Important Thing to Remember

If, when you talk to members of the Safety Squad and ask them how you can work together and they say you can't, remember one thing. You're the boss. Even if the Safety Squad is still strident and critical (which at this point I hope they aren't as much), remembering that they are just trying to keep you safe may help temper their impact. They are like having untrained guard dogs who sometimes get confused and bite you instead of the enemy. As you engage, they calm down. In the meantime, remember you have the ultimate say about the role they play in your life.

"Art is not
what you see,
but what you
make others see."
~ Edgar Degas

Photo by Sahand Hoseini on Unsplash

TWELVE

Show Me The Money

I MEAN THIS IN THE
NICEST POSSIBLE WAY.

People Need Help to Buy

Make buying from you as easy as you can. If possible, set up your website so your people can click to buy, pay, and handle shipping right there. This is how everyone expects to be able to purchase everything now. Often (maybe because the Jailer is active), artists want people to direct message them to get prices and to arrange a purchase. Maybe in a parallel universe this happens, but mostly, people won't message you. It's too time-consuming. It's also risky for people to talk directly to a real artist.

We Aren't the Only Ones With Money Issues.

Our people may have them too. They might not want to discuss your pricing with you any more than you want to with them. There are so many apps that make the process of buying simple and private. Help your people who feel embarrassed about discussing money with you by using one of these apps on your website.

The other way to help people buy is to sell things that range in price. Offering work in a range of prices will make it easier for your people to take a risk on you.

How to Remove the Risk of Trying Something New

For most people, spending even small amounts of money to hear a new band, buy a piece of art online, purchase tickets to an unknown play, or see a dance company for the first time, is risky. We don't trust our own taste. Many people find it much easier (but way less satisfying) to buy a print off the wall at a chain furniture store, watch the #1 trending movie, or stream one of the top 10 hits, anointed by some "authority," than buy something from you.

Your people need help with the risk they feel in buying from you, especially first-time buyers. You can reduce their risk by selling things that range in price, including some things that are relatively inexpensive, or if your art lends itself to this, providing downloads or samples. This helps people ease into the relationship and gives you both a foundation to build on.

Now...Pricing

This brings up the matter of setting prices for your work. Take a couple of deep breaths before you begin reading this, in case you have some fear or previous trauma around pricing. There are three simple ways to set prices for your art, and you already know everything you need to know to use any of them.

Pricing By the Hour

The first way is to price your work based on how many hours it took to create it. If you want to make $100 per hour and it took you ten hours to make something, then you could consider charging $100 X 10 = $1,000 for it. This method can work if you are painting, sculpting, doing ceramics or making anything physical.

Your Time Matters

If you price this way, watch out for two pitfalls. First, sometimes artists think the only thing that matters when they're making something physical is the cost of the materials. Their time is free. A sculptor in one of my classes spent 36 hours carving a gorgeous eagle which she sold for $250. That's $6.94 per hour, not including the cost of the wood, which was about $30. Disregarding her time, she calculated that she made $220 on the piece, (sale price of $250 minus the $30 for materials) which she didn't think was terrible. But when we did the math to include her time, she cried. This is a textbook example of why considering the cost of materials alone won't produce the right price.

All Your Time Matters

The other pitfall is not considering *all* the time it takes to make something. If you're a musician, you may routinely assume (as do the people who hire you) that you only get paid for the performance. Practice and rehearsals don't count. If you teach groups of people, you might assume that the price you charge them only takes into consideration the time you spend teaching, disregarding your prep time. If you put on live events, you might want to disregard the cost of the administrative time it took to set up and run the event. If you paint large scale public art, you may be tempted to charge only for the time you're actually painting, ignoring the design time, the back-and-forth with the client, getting permits from the city, and the hundred other time-intensive activities that have to happen before you can lift your paintbrush.

Clarity Is the Key

There are no right or wrong answers in pricing your work by the hour, or which hours you include (prep, practice, etc.) in the total hours you charge for. Whether you include the set-up, planning, communicating, tear-down and behind-the-scenes hours or not, it's good practice to see how many hours there are. Then you can consciously decide if you want to include them or not.

If pricing your creative work by the hour seems right for you, see what happens when you multiply the hours you spend making, practicing, and delivering it, by an hourly rate you realistically want to earn.

What Is the "Going Rate?"

The next way is to charge what other people charge for similar work. The internet is bursting with pricing information. You can price a painting by the square inch, tempered by how long you've been painting and how much work you've sold. If you're a musician people will tell you what they pay for a gig, and you can always talk to other musicians. If you self-publish books, you can easily research what books in your genre cost on Amazon.

"Creativity
takes courage."
~ Henri Matisse

The Downside: There Is No "Going Rate"

This method has one pitfall. When you start researching what other people are charging, you'll find enormous, mystifying variations. Even prices for everyday items like toothpaste, fruit, shoes, probably every product or service out there can vary by hundreds, sometimes thousands of dollars. A pair of Yubari King melons (a type of rare cantaloupe) sold at auction in Japan in 2016 for $27,000. It's possible to get a $.99 book or a $95 edition. And it's possible to sell a $50 photograph or a $50,000 one. The information you discover from researching what other people charge won't completely solve your pricing problem, but it will make you more informed and give you a place to start.

What Does Your Gut Say?

The third way to price is by listening to your gut.

This method works the best when you've already sold something. Often when you sell something you'll realize, based on how you felt before, during and after the transaction, that it was too cheap. Sometimes people feel like they charged too much, but in my experience that's rare. We underprice more often, by far.

Here's how the "use your gut" method works.

1. Pick something you do or make and set a price for it.
2. Check your gut.
3. If your gut says, "Sure, that's fine," then raise the price and check again.
4. If it says, "OH HELL NO," then lower your price and check again.
5. If it says, "Okay, maybe, scary, but possibly doable," then that's your price.

Sell to the Right People

The "use your gut" method comes with two pitfalls. The first one will emerge if you choose the wrong people to sell to. You can collect completely erroneous information by selling things to family and friends or just the wrong people altogether, ranging from "I'd pay big bucks for ***anything*** you do," to people at art fairs who say, "That's too expensive," or "I could make that myself." Unless the fair is juried and held in Beverly Hills, the people who attend art fairs think everything should cost less than $10. The bottom line: make sure you're getting feedback from your right people.

Standing In Your Own Worth

The other pitfall comes from the difficulty you might have realizing your own value. This difficulty creates an idea in your head that can also derail the other two pricing methods. If you struggle to see your own value, you might decide that the time you put into something doesn't matter, or that you have to charge at the bottom end of the going rate. If you don't recognize your own value, you'll also tend to set your prices too low using your gut.

This is most likely the Safety Squad at work, particularly the Judge. The solution is more peace talks. Start with this question, "When you criticize my worth as an artist, what is your motivation?" You'll get some insight into why the Judge believes criticizing your worth is a good idea, and you can take steps to calm it down so you can see the truth.

The Universal Magic Cure for Everything

The antidote to this, and to all other problems that come up when you think about pricing your work, is to go back and look at the work you did to understand who your people are, what they want from you, and how they want to feel when they buy your work. You can also go back and review the conversation with your Mentor about the purpose of your art. Both tasks will remind you who you are, why you do what you do, who wants and needs what you create, and most importantly, why it matters.

Which method should you use? The one that speaks to you. Or you can combine them. Do some research about what other people charge, then use your gut. Or figure out what the price would be if you charged by the hour, then check your gut.

Luckily, this is an experiment. You can change your prices any time, and over time, as you practice your craft and get better, you should change them. They should go up.

Your Work Matters

It's easy to feel overwhelmed by all this. The key to managing overwhelm is to remember that this is an unfolding process; take baby steps and keep the purpose of your art uppermost in your mind. When you keep your purpose in mind while you get visible, make relationships with your people and help them buy, you remember why all this is important, even vital. Your work matters. People need it. No one else but you can make it.

AFTER

Unstuck, Confident, Decisive, Bold

An artist sits down to make something. As advised by the Jellyfish who was happy to tell her which task she should do that would free her mind to create, she stuck a load of laundry in the washer. She'd just run out of clean underwear and the Jellyfish knew she'd obsess about it if she didn't handle that first.

As she readies her workspace, her Muse, the owl, flies in through the open window. The owl is clutching the piece of paper in her talons and drops it next to the artist.

"Thanks," says the artist. "I was hoping you'd show up with more ideas."

"I always do. Let's look at them and see which one you want to start on first." They put their heads together to discuss which ideas appeal most.

They pick one and the owl-Muse flies over to sit on her perch to rest. "Wake me up if you need more ideas."

As the artist picks up her tools, the Maker appears next. "I've got some suggestions for you," he says. They chat about ways to start the project, which materials the artist might need, and how to finish. "Looks like you're set," says the Maker, as they wind up their conversation. "I'll be resting on the couch. Call if you need me."

The artist works on the creation for a while, then hits a stuck point.

Her Mentor materializes in the chair next to her. "No worries," says the Mentor, "Let's go back and discuss the purpose of this work, and the overall purpose of your art." They talk for a few minutes. The stuck point gradually releases. "Call me when you need me again," says the Mentor.

The artist works a bit longer. She realizes, as the Judge told her, she needs feedback on what she's made so far from someone who is knowledgeable about her work. The Judge also suggested the person who would be a good source of constructive, helpful, kind feedback, and she makes an appointment to talk to that person the following day.

Over the next few days, and with the practical feedback from her colleague, she finishes the work and posts it on her social media account and her website.

One of her followers makes a snarky comment about it.

"Ignore them," advises the Jailer. "People like that aren't your people. In fact, you can block that person if you want. You need to be seen by people who appreciate what you're doing. Ignore everyone else. They don't matter." The artist smiles to herself as she blocks the detractor.

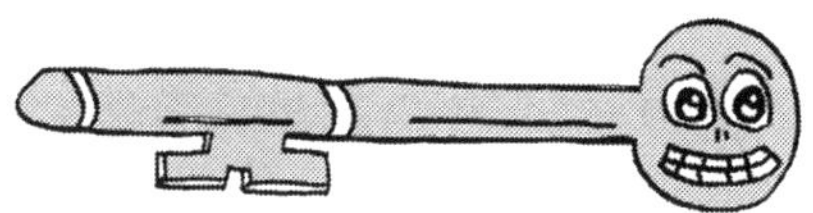

Over the weeks and months, the artist finishes more and more work. She sets aside time every week to dialog with the Mentor about how to talk about the work, how to tell the story of each piece—how she came to make them, what they mean, how they make her feel. She posts the work on her website, talks about all of it to her people, and they begin to buy.

When the artist resists starting something new, she checks in with the Jellyfish to see if there are any tasks she truly needs to take care of, or if the Jellyfish just needs some reassurance that it's safe to create.

When she needs more ideas, she talks to her Muse.

When she needs to solve a problem with her craft, she brainstorms with the Maker.

The Mentor knows where to post information about her work and what to say. The Jailer might speak up if she gets a critical comment from someone and will suggest ignoring or blocking them. When she hears the Judge in her head commenting on something she made, she stops to listen. Because of her peaceful relationship with the Judge, she knows he's trying to protect her and will provide helpful advice. She also knows that if the advice swings into critical territory that she's the boss; she can listen, not listen, or come back later when the Judge is in a better mood.

And the Mentor, in touch with her purpose, her projects and the certainty of the importance of her work in the world, is an endless source of clarity, encouragement and inspiration.

Will It Be Like This Every Day?

No. But as you make friends with the Safety Squad you begin to see how its sole motivation is to protect you. Once you see that, the path to friendship and peace with the Squad has begun to be paved.

As you consult with the Creative Council, you strengthen your connection to the parts of your brain that know what you're up to and know how to do it. You begin experiencing what it's like to trust yourself.

You've found the way to make peace with your brain and money + joy with your art. You remember who you are, what you're up to, why it matters, and how brilliant, creative, and necessary your art is. This is true prosperity.

Acknowledgements

Every book acknowledgment starts by recognizing this immutable fact: no author ever finishes a book alone. This book is no exception.

Mary Palumbo, long deceased, introduced me to Carl Jung and the concept of parts work, over thirty years ago. She set me on a journey to discover just what was driving my behavior that continues to this day. Jeffrey Van Dyk and Pat Honiotes taught me how to use parts work in a business setting; I benefited from Beth Scanzani's profound expertise in parts work and her teaching me how to use it with clients.

Michelle Radomski's book birthing process helped this book grow from an acorn to an oak. She held a vision for it throughout the three years it took to write, never fearing to send me back to revise it with, "You're close, but this isn't quite it yet." She was always right. We also wanted this book to look creative and accessible. The finished product is a result of her insightful guidance, intuition, and exceptional design skill.

The artists Lori Johnson, Kathryn Mitchell, Emily Gonzales, and Willow Paule read and used early versions and helped me refine my initial ideas. Sam Beasley and Elizabeth Treanor calmed and encouraged me when I didn't think I could or would finish and showed me how to fund my own art with money and time. Suzanne Lorenz provided inspiration and feedback. Carol Booton and I spent hours brainstorming about how to talk to artists about money without sending them fleeing for the exits. Moe Bell provided creative ideas about how to incorporate my clients' work in the book.

I am indebted to the many clients who motivated me to look deeper into why brilliant, creative people struggled with money, resistance, the inner critic, and visibility, and to arrive at a simple (if not easy) solution to that problem.

I wanted this book to include cartoons, but when I started the book, I couldn't draw. I wanted to see if I could learn how to draw believable representations of the characters in the book, and experience what you, my precious readers feel when you begin doing a new kind of art and aren't very good at it. I took a cartooning class, then individual lessons from Tom Motley, instructor and cartoonist extraordinaire, and was surprised to find myself showing up to the first few lessons crying in fear and frustration. Tom reminded me of my own advice about what to do when the Safety Squad showed up in full voice, which it did; edited the drawings to correct my most egregious mistakes, and used his industrial magic to shade the drawings when we finished them. Neither the drawings nor the courage to use them in the book would have happened without him.

The Diamond Approach and its teachers, along with my fellow students, introduced me to inquiry, a compassionate way to get to know my inner critic.

Finally, conducting peace talks with my own inner critic the way I've outlined them in this book, continue to work. My inner critic has evolved from being loud and terrified into a keen-eyed (if occasionally still loud) ally and guide. Thank you for your unflagging support.

About the Author

By day, Christy Strauch is the Possibility to Profit coach. She helps creatives turn their chaotic pile of creative possibilities into a profitable business. She is the author of three books, plus *Artists: Prosper!* and an accompanying workbook, *Artists Unstuck!*

This book is the result of clients telling her they were too creative to handle money, and her realizing that handling money required second grade math. There had to be something else operating here; the answer to which is the subject of the book.

She also knew destiny was involved in writing *Artists: Prosper!* because her own inner critic was so persistent, loud, and, well, critical. Conducting peace talks with it as outlined in this book, she and her inner critic have negotiated a permanent cease-fire.

By night she is a dedicated beginner ukulele player and traveler. She lives peacefully in Arizona, surrounded by beautiful art, shelves of books, and a view of Camelback Mountain.

Made in the USA
Columbia, SC
06 December 2021

50233139R00083